A Daybook for January

In Yellow Springs, Ohio

A Memoir in Nature

and a Handbook for the Month, Being a Personal Narrative and Synthesis of Common Events in Nature between 1981 and 2023 in Southwestern Ohio, with Applications for the Lower Midwest and Middle Atlantic Region, Containing Weather Guidelines and a Variety of Natural Calendars, Reflections by the Author and Seasonal Quotations from Ancient and Modern Writers

By

Bill Felker

A Daybook for the Year in Yellow Springs, Ohio
Volume 1: January

Cover from a watercolor by Libby Rudolf

Copyright 2023 by Bill Felker

Published by The Green Thrush Press
P.O. Box 431, Yellow Springs, Ohio

Printed in the United States of America
Charleston, SC

ISBN-9781728671352

For Jeni

No one suspects the days to be gods.

Ralph Waldo Emerson

Introduction

Here are no stories told you of what is to be seen at the other end of the world, but of things at home, in your own Native Countrey, at your own doors, easily examinable with little travel, less cost, and very little hazard. This book doth not shew you a Telescope, but a Mirror, it goes not about to put a delightful cheat upon you, with objects at a great distance, but shews you yourselves.

Joshua Childrey, 1660

This memoir is a record of everyday walks in fields and woods, a journal of losing myself in finding and watching, an exploration of what it means for me to live in in southwestern Ohio. I have gathered here quotations about time and nature, essays from my column in the local newspaper, meteorological commentary made up from my lengthy obsession with tracking the weather, notes about common events in nature, syntheses of these events, and astronomical information based on my years of writing almanacs. Although I have organized my work on a scaffolding of back-yard natural history and observation, I am not a naturalist and have had no training in the natural sciences. All of what is contained in the *Daybook* is the result of my search for myself and for meaning.

This particular aspect of my search began in 1972 with the gift of a barometer. My wife, Jeanie, gave the instrument to me when I was succumbing to graduate school stress in Knoxville, Tennessee, and it became not only an escape from intense academic work, but the first step on the road to a different kind of awareness about the world.

From the start, I was never content just to watch the barometric needle; I had to record its movement, then graph it. I was fascinated by the alchemy of the charts that turned rain and Sun into visible patterns, symbols like notes on a sheet of music, or words on a page.

From my graphs of barometric pressure, I discovered that the number of cold fronts each month is more or less consistent, and that the Earth breathes at an average rate of about once every three to five days in the winter, and once each six to eight days at the peak of summer.

A short apprenticeship told me when important changes would occur and what kind of weather would take place on most any day. That information was expressed in the language of odds and percentages, and it was surprisingly accurate. Taking into consideration the consistency of certain patterns in the past, I could make fairly successful predictions about the likelihood of the repetition of such paradigms in the future. As Yeats says, the seasons "have their fixed returns," and I found points all along the course of the year which appeared to be fixed moments for change. The pulse of the world was steadier than I had ever imagined.

My graphs also allowed me to see the special properties of each season. August's barometric configurations, for example, are slow and gentle like low, rolling hills. Heat waves show up as plateaus. Thunderstorms are sharp, shallow troughs in the gentle waves of the atmospheric landscape. Autumn arrives like the sudden appearance of a pyramid on a broad plain. By the end of September, the fronts are stronger; the high-pressure peaks become taller; the lows are deeper, with almost every valley bringing rain. By December, the systems loom on the horizon of the graph like a range of mountains with violent extremes of altitude, sometimes snowcapped, almost always imposing and sliced by canyons of wind.

From watching the weather, it was an easy step to watching wildflowers. Identifying plants, I saw that flowers were natural allies of my graphs, and that they were parallel measures of the seasons and the passage of time. I kept a list of when each wildflower blossomed and saw how each one consistently opened around a specific day, and that even though a cold year could set blooming back up to two weeks, and unusual warmth accelerate it, average dates were quite useful in establishing sequence of bloom which always showed me exactly where I was in the progress of the year.

In the summer of 1978, Jeanie and I took the family to Yellow Springs, Ohio, a small town just beyond the eastern edge of the Dayton suburbs. We bought a house and planned to stay. I began to write a nature almanac for the local newspaper. To my weather and wildflower notes I added daily sunrise and sunset times, moonrise and moonset, average and record temperatures, comments on foliage changes, bird migration dates, farm and gardening cycles, and the rotation of the stars. The more I learned around Yellow Springs, the more I found applicable to the world beyond the village limits. The microclimate in which I immersed myself gradually became a key to the extended environment; the part unlocked the whole. My Yellow Springs gnomon that measured the movement of the Sun also measured my relationship to every other place on earth.

My occasional trips turned into exercises in the measurement of variations in the landscape. When I drove 500 miles northwest, I not only entered a different space, but often a separate season, and I could mark the differences in degrees of flowers, insects, trees, and the development of the field crops. The most exciting trips were taken south in March; I could travel from Early Spring into Middle Spring and finally into Late Spring and summer along the Gulf Coast.

My engagement with the natural world, which began as an escape from academia, finally turned into a way of getting private bearings and of finding what I loved and believed. It was a process of spiritual as well as physical reorientation. In that way, all the historical statements in this collection of notes are the fruit of a strong desire to define where I am and what happens around me.

The Daybook Format

The format of my notes in this daybook owes more than a little to the almanacs I wrote for the *Yellow Springs News* between 1984 and 2017. The quotations, daily statistics, the weather outlooks, the seasonal calendar, and the daybook entries were and still are part of my regular routine of collecting and organizing impressions about the place in which I live.

Setting: The principal habitat described here is that of Glen Helen, a preserve of woods and glades that lies on the eastern border of the village of Yellow Springs in southwestern Ohio. At its northern edge, the Glen joins with John Bryan State Park to form a corridor about ten miles long, and half a mile wide, along the Little Miami River. The north section of the Glen Helen /John Bryan complex is hilly and heavily wooded, and is the best location for spring wildflowers. The southern portion, "South Glen" as it is usually called, is a combination of open fields, wetlands, and wooded flatlands. Here I found many flowers and grasses of summer and fall. Together, the two Glens and John Bryan Park provide a remarkable cross section of the fauna and flora of the eastern United States.

Other habitats in the daybook include my yard with its several small gardens; the village of Yellow Springs itself, a town of 4,000 at the far eastern border of the Dayton suburbs; the Caesar Creek Reservoir, twenty miles south of Yellow Springs and created by the Corps of Engineers in 1976. My trips away from that environment were principally northeast to Chicago, Madison, Wisconsin and northern Minnesota, east to Washington and New York, southeast to the Carolinas and Florida, southwest to Arkansas, Louisiana, and Texas, and occasionally through the Southwest to California and the Northwest, two excursions to Belize in Central America, several to Italy.

Quotations: The passages from ancient and modern writers (and sometimes from my alter egos) which accompany each day's notations are lessons from my readings, as well as from distant seminary and university training, here put to work in service of the reconstruction of my sense of time and space. They are a collection of reminders, hopes, and promises for me that I find implicit in the seasons. They have also become a kind of a cosmological scrapbook for me, as well as the philosophical underpinning of this narrative.

Astronomical Data: The *Daybook* includes approximate dates for astronomical events, such as star positions, meteor showers, solstice, equinox, perihelion (the Sun's position closest to earth), and aphelion (the Sun's position farthest from Earth).

I have included the sunrise and sunset for Yellow Springs as a general guide to the progression of the year in this location, but those statistics also reflect trends that are world wide, if more rapid in some places and slower in others.

Even though the day's length is almost never exactly the same from one town to the next, a minute gained or lost in Yellow Springs is often a minute lost or gained elsewhere, and the Yellow

Springs numbers can be used as a simple way of watching the lengthening or shortening of the days, and, therefore, of watching the turn of the planet. For those who wish to keep track of the Sun themselves in their own location, abundant sources are now available for this information in local and national media.

Average Temperatures: Average temperatures in Yellow Springs are also part of each day's entry. Since the rise and fall of temperatures in other parts of the North America, even though they may start from colder or warmer readings, keep pace with the temperatures here, the highs and lows in Yellow Springs are, like solar statistics, helpful indicators of the steady progress of the year throughout most of the states along the 40th Parallel (except in the mountains). The daybook entries can be cross-referenced with the list of monthly average temperatures between 1981 and 2017 in order to compare the daily inventories with the month's weather in a given year.

Weather: My daily, weekly and monthly weather summaries have been distilled from over thirty years of observations. They are descriptions of the local weather history I have kept in order to track the gradual change in temperatures, precipitation and cloud cover through the year I have also used them in order to try to identify particular characteristics of each day. They are not meant to be predictions.

Although my interest in the Yellow Springs microclimate at first seemed too narrow to be of use to those who lived outside the area, I began to modify it to meet the needs of a number of regional and national farm publications for which I started writing in the mid 1980s. And so, while the summaries are based on my records in southwestern Ohio, they can be and have been used, with interpretation and interpolation, throughout the Lower Midwest , the Middle Atlantic States and the East.

The Natural Calendar: In this section, I note the progress of foliage and floral changes, farm and garden practices, migration times for common birds, and peak periods of insect activity. Some of these notes are second hand; I'm a sky watcher, but not an astronomer, and I rely on the government's astronomical data and a few other references for much of my information about the stars and the sun. I am also a complete amateur at bird watching, and most of the migration dates used in the seasonal calendar come from published sources. And even though I keep close track of the farm year, the percentages listed for planting and harvesting are interpretations of averages supplied by the state's weekly crop reports.

Daybook Entries: The entries in the daybook section provide the raw material from which I wrote the Natural Calendar digests. The daybook section is a collection of observations made from the window of my car and from my walks in Glen Helen, in parks and wildlife areas within a few miles of my home, and on occasional trips. It is a record that anyone with a few guidebooks could make, and it includes just a small number of the natural markers that anyone might discover.

When I began to take notes about the world around me, I found that there were few descriptions of actual events in nature available for southwestern Ohio. There was no roadmap for the course of the year. My daily observations, as narrow and incomplete as they were, were especially significant to me since I had found no other narrative of the days, no other depiction of what was actually occurring around me. In time, the world came into focus with each particle I named. I saw concretely that time and space were the sum of their parts.

As my notes for each day accumulated, I could see the wide variation of events that occurred from year to year; at the same time, I saw a unity in this syncopation from which I could identify numerous sub-seasons and with which I could understand better the kind of habitat in which I was living and, consequently, myself.

When I paged through the entries for each day, I was drawn back to the space in which they were made. I browsed and imagined, returned to the journey.

Journal Essays: At the end of many of the daybook entries, I have included brief essays from my almanac column in the *Dayton Daily News*.

Companions: Many friends, acquaintances and family members have contributed their observations to the daybook, and their participation has taught me that my private seasons are also community seasons, and that all of our experiences together help to lay the foundation for a rich, local consciousness of natural history.

*** The Month of January ***
January Averages: 1981 through 2023
Normal January Average Temperature: 27.5

Year	Average
1981	23.3
1982	20.9
1983	29.1
1984	21.2
1985	19.9
1986	29.1
1987	28.2
1988	26.1
1989	36.3
1990	37.1
1991	28.1
1992	30.0
1993	32.1
1994	20.0
1995	28.9
1996	25.0
1997	25.7
1998	36.0
1999	28.8
2000	24.9
2001	28.1
2002	34.4
2003	20.7
2004	23.5
2005	28.5
2006	38.9
2007	32.3
2008	28.4
2009	21.2
2010	24.3
2011	22.9
2012	30.7
2013	30.6
2014	21.3
2015	26.6
2016	27.9
2017	34.4
2018	25.7
2019	28.5
2020	36.1
2021	32.1
2022	25.4
2023	.37.4

***January 1st**
The 1st Day of the Year*

Yea, this is the hardest month of all:
Hard for men and women,
Hard for beasts as well.

Hesiod

Sunrise/set: 7:57/5:21
Day's Length: 9 hours 24 minutes
Average High/Low: 36/20
Average Temperature: 28
Record High: 61 – 1952
Record Low: - 8 – 1968, -7 – 2018

The Daily Weather
About twice in every decade, today is mild, reaching into the 40s or 50s; otherwise the first day of the year is in the 20s or 30s. A morning below zero is rare, although 85 percent of the dawns dip below freezing. Skies remain completely cloudy half the years in my record. When precipitation occurs, it often precedes the windy first cold front of Deep Winter.

The January Outlook for Southwestern Ohio
and the Lower Midwest
Precipitation almost always precedes the seven cold waves that strike this month. Snow falls at least three times, and as many as ten times.

Normal highs begin near 36 on January 1. They drop to 35 the following day, and they reach their lowest point of the year, 34 degrees, on January 10. Average low temperatures fall to 18 around that time, and there is no improvement in the situation until the 28th of the month.

January usually produces an average of nine days in the 20s, three days with highs only in the teens, and one day when the temperature does not get above ten degrees. There is almost always one mild day during the month, sometimes up to ten. About 12 days are in the 30s, and there can be up to five days in the 40s and

50s. An average of two mornings dip below zero (the 9th and the 11th being the days most likely to see such cold).

There are ten to 15 afternoons when highs stay below freezing, and often those days come together, creating the definitive freeze of middle winter. The worst spells fall between the 1st and the 20th. Major storms are most likely to occur around January 1, 8-12, and 19-24.

Wintercount

Major January weather systems cross the country at the rate of one major cold wave about every five days. Occasionally, two fronts come back to back, intensifying the severity of conditions. Two or three days of colder weather accompany the arrival of each front; they are followed by about two days of moderating temperatures. Although such warming times are typical, January can provide up to ten or 15 days in a row during which temperatures remain below normal.

January 1: The New Year's front is usually one of the most severe systems so far in the winter, and it is preceded by sleet or snow as far south as northern Florida. After its passage, temperatures are typically quite cold. A secondary disturbance often causes additional precipitation on the 2nd and 3rd.

January 5: As the year's second major front approaches, milder temperatures and more precipitation are likely; thunderstorms are not uncommon in the South. After the January 5th high passes through, however, the cold returns, and the 8th and 9th are associated with some of the most chilling weather so far in the winter.

January 10: The period between January 8th and 12th is one of the main storm windows of year. Not only are blizzards most likely to occur at this time during the first half of the month, but below-zero morning lows are most likely to occur. With a continuing increase in the cold, skies have fewer clouds, and the 12th and 13th bring a better-than-average chance of sun to the eastern half of the nation.

January 15: The day prior to this front is very likely to bring clouds and precipitation. After its passage, the January 15th front initiates a two-week period during which average temperatures are the lowest of the year. Days on which the temperature does not rise above zero typically occur more often this week than any other week, and morning lows below zero occur after the January 15th front more often than at any other time. But after this high moves east, the chances of a slight warm-up increase. During January's third week in 1890, one of the longest record-breaking thaws in weather history warmed temperatures into the 60s for three days across the Midwest.

January 19: Although the United States lies in the middle of its most frigid time of the entire year, the possibility of mild weather is enhanced by the incursion of powerful southerly winds from the Gulf of Mexico. The resulting turbulence often creates the "January Thaw," a brief space during which much milder temperatures and an increased likelihood of blizzards, thunderstorms, tornados and flooding occurs. After the passage of the January 19th front, the average chances of cold increase for a day or two, then fall off slowly, sometimes never recovering their mid-winter strength. Low barometric pressure before the arrival of the next weather system increases the likelihood of mild conditions.

January 25: This front spawns storms, accompanied by snow or rain, and the days following its arrival make the 25th and 26th some of the month's chillier days. Secondary frontal conditions, sometimes carrying moist Gulf air, can set off powerful blizzards around the 27th. Most years, however, the sun shines and makes the 27th one of the brightest days of the month. The 27th is also a pivotal statistical date in the fortunes of winter. Throughout the country average temperatures, which had remained stable from the middle of January, climb one degree. That rise may not be obvious in any particular year, but it does represent the cumulative wisdom of all the years on record, revealing the inevitable turn of the Earth toward June. The January 27th shift also signals the advent of Late Winter, a period that still may bring terrible cold and storms but which, overall, paves the way for Early Spring.

January 31: This is the second weather system of Late Winter, and it is typically followed by an even more pronounced thaw than occurred after the previous two fronts.

*** Key to the Nation's Weather ***

The typical January temperature at average elevations along the 40th Parallel, the average of the high of 38 and the low of 22, is 30 degrees. Using the following chart based on weather statistics from around the country, one can calculate approximate temperatures in locations close to the cities listed.

For example, with the average of the 40th Parallel as the base of 30, you can estimate normal temperatures in Minneapolis by subtracting 18 degrees from the base average. Or add 12 degrees to find out the likely conditions in Raleigh during the month.

Minneapolis	-18
Green Bay	-13
Burlington VT	-12
Des Moines	-9
Chicago	-4
Pittsburgh	-1
AVERAGE ALONG 40TH PARALLEL	**30**
St. Louis	+2
New York	+4
Louisville	+6
Washington DC	+7
Atlanta	+15
Miami	+35

*** January Phenology ***

When white-tailed bucks start to lose their antlers in the North, then yellow Jessamine is blooming along the Gulf Coast, camellias are at their best there; avocados and papayas are ripening.

When the first crocus leaves push up in milder years, then the first pussy willow catkin could be open just a crack.

When pine trees pollinate, then owls are nesting in the wood lots.

When daffodil foliage is an inch tall in Chicago, then Algerian iris will soon be blossoming in Virginia. Aconites and snowdrops begin to bloom in the Carolinas.

When pale Asian ladybugs emerge in the warmth of

sunny windowsills, then nurseries and grocery stores set up spring flower displays.

When crows migrate, then the sun has moved into Aquarius and the January thaw is right around the corner.

When the first fly gets inside your house, then opossums and skunks wander the woods at night.

When cardinals sing before dawn, Late Winter has begun. Although this period can be one of the coldest of the year in the North, its thaws accelerate the swelling of buds and the blooming of early bulbs across the South and Border States.

The Natural Calendar

The Season of Deep Winter, the second major phase of the year's coldest time, ordinarily begins on January 1 and lasts three weeks. In the greenhouse, the Season of Jade Tree Bloom wanes as Camellia Season flowers in the Deep South and Black Bear Hibernation Season ends in southern forests. Throughout much of North America, Fox Mating Season and Coyote Mating Season take place beside Owl Nesting Season. Pine Pollination Season adds pine pollen to the south winds. Sparrows become even louder as Sparrow Courting Season follows the lengthening days.

The most bitter time of the year is not the darkest time. In Early Winter, sunset became later by ten minutes from its earliest time, and the sun's declination started to surge. Now the night contracts at the rate of about 90 seconds every day, moving from 9 hours 24 minutes on January 1 to 10 hours and 6 minutes on the last day of the month.

The crows have already marked the far reach of dawn to its latest incursion of the year, keeping vigil over the progress of the sun, measuring the passage of winter with their calls, waking titmice and then the cardinals at Deep Winter's close.

The seasonal clock has advanced by the span of one moon since the last leaves fell to the ground. The first weeds and wildflowers were already rising slowly through November and December: hemlock, lamium, garlic mustard, creeping Charlie, sweet rockets, sweet Cicely, dock, skunk cabbage, wood mint, watercress, mouse-eared chickweed. Tips of snowdrops and snow crocus had sometimes emerged.

Here at the beginning of Deep Winter, it is not too late to

sink a ruler against a few these plants to track their upward progress. And it is the time to start a daily count of how many pussy willow catkins have started to unfold. Five major cold fronts of Early Winter have already come and gone. Six major cold fronts of Deep Winter will pass through about every five days like strokes of a pendulum, often leaving thaw in their wake, pulling open the catkins, tugging on the foliage waiting in the ground.

When the Natural Year began in early December, Orion lay at the eastern horizon before midnight, marking one phase of star-time for the new cycle. It moves west in the dark throughout Deep and Late Winter; setting on April evenings, it heralds Middle Spring. Rising in the east early on June mornings, passing due south at high noon during summer's Dog Days, it returns to the evening sky as the falling leaves bring an end to Late Autumn.

Today through the 10th are the days with the year's latest sunrise along the 40th Parallel. Sunset, however, continues to occur a minute or two later each day this month, and the day's length in Yellow Springs increases during January from nine hours 24 minutes to ten hours and ten minutes.

The Weather in the Week Ahead
The warmest days of January's first quarter are typically the 3rd and the 6th, each having a 25 percent chance of highs in the 40s or 50s. Cold comes too, however. The first major cold front of the year arrives the last day of December or the 1st or 2nd of January, and most days between the 1st and the 7th have a 30 to 40 percent chance of highs only in the 20s or teens. The 8th and 9th, which coincide with the arrival of the year's second major weather system, have the coldest records of all, each with a 50 to 55 percent chance of highs below 30. Clouds usually dominate the sky this week: there is just a 40 percent chance of sun between the 1st and 3rd, and there is even a 70 percent chance of completely overcast conditions on the 6th. Precipitation is lightest on the 1st (a 30 percent chance), but heaviest on the 2nd and 3rd (around a 50 percent chance). Chances of other days this week are in the 40 percent range.

Daybook
1982: Today the composition of winter seems plain and distinct.

The absence of migratory birds magnifies the rattle of the downy woodpecker and the calling of the crows. Nothing is concealed by foliage. The natural year is complete and therefore finite and countable. Now there's enough time to look at everything. I can list remnants at leisure. I can rebuild the summer and document spring's progress with simple, reassuring measurements.

This afternoon was quiet and cold. The black centers of the empty milkweed pods faced the sun. Thistle and garlic mustard, still green, clustered close to the ground. Osage fruits were open, shredded by the squirrels. The seed heads of ironweed were pale and soft, their stalks hung with love vine by the swamp.

There were ducks on the river, no ice yet, even along the sloughs. I saw black-capped chickadees, a flicker, four titmice, three silent cardinals, white sycamores, some orange honeysuckle berries still left, red rose hips, broken, dark angelica. Doves scattered when I walked through the goldenrod. Skunk cabbage was up at the swamp past the Covered Bridge.

I counted the pussy willows that were opening. I fingered the seed heads of the New England asters to see if all the seeds were gone. I kicked the fat Osage fruits to understand how they were doing: they are chartreuse green when they tumble down in October and November, turn yellower and yellower through the fall, start to get mushy in the middle of winter, fall apart in spring.

I found the plants that keep their green through the coldest times - the hellebores, the creeping charley, the chickweed and pachysandra, garlic mustard, mullein, sweet rocket, and sweet William, and I was reassured by their deep color and hardiness.

Tonight, the sun went down a full ten minutes later than it did two weeks ago. Orion was in the east after supper, the Pleiades overhead, red Taurus between them. The Northern Cross was setting over Dayton. Sirius came up an hour before midnight.

1983: Crocus leaves are still growing in the south garden, as is the foliage of columbine, purple deadnettle, catnip, forget- me-not, garlic mustard, dandelion, wild onion, celandine, and henbit.

1985: At the Covered Bridge, 59 degrees, wind and rain, barometer falling sharply: skunk cabbage is up in the swamp, the tallest spears about three inches but not blooming. New mint is common here, water cress bright. Some dock, chickweed, catchweed found. The river is high. No insects seen. Squirrels are out, continuing to shred Osage fruits. In the yard this afternoon, I saw five squirrels chasing each other in the biggest locust. Mating ritual? In the garden, two purple deadnettle plants have violet blossoms.

1986: Two weeks of early middle winter have left only a few bittersweet fruits hanging on their vine.

1987: Barometer falling, 37 degrees: A huge flock of geese flew over North Glen at 9:15 a.m. Seven chubs and a shiner brought home from Sycamore Hole, all about eight inches long. Small fish bit from 3:30 to 5:00 this afternoon, probably two dozen caught close to shore on dough balls. Bobwhite heard late, calling from the other side of the water. Geese flew over the house at 4:35 p.m. and 4:45 p.m.

1988: South Glen, 25 degrees and sun: Three bluebirds seen up from Sycamore Hole. Winter cress, thistle, mullein, and red clover are all bright green in the clipped field by the red barn. A little ice on the edges of the river. Milkweed pods are completely empty now. Squirrels active in the sun. A downy woodpecker climbs up and down on the wingstem a couple of yards from me.

1989: Cardinals singing on and off in the afternoon sun.

1991: South Glen: The woods quiet, a woodpecker heard only once. Flood waters down, but the river still maybe a foot or two above normal. Last week, the water came up over the path and reached all the way to Jacoby Road. At some points along the shore, the flood went in hundreds of yards, and the ground is still soft from the soaking. Leaves are pressed against the Osage, multiflora roses, sapling buckeyes, the sycamores, maple, box elder. Sand has been swept up into the prairie, trees fallen from their own waterlogged weight, logs washed inland. Where the water still stands, there is the smell of sewage from the overburdened treatment plant upstream.

1999: Single-digit cold, the house quiet, no wind, greenhouse glass frosted, no crows or cardinals, half an inch of snow on the ground. The pond heater is keeping the east corner of the water open. Inside, the jade trees bloom here and there, and the mother-of-millions are budding. The tomatoes are producing heavily, will provide all of January's sandwiches and pastas. At 8:14 a.m., the first crows call from the trees in the west lot. Sparrows start chirping at 8:20. The sky clouds up this afternoon, even as the barometer is rising, and a major weather system approaches; it's due within twelve hours or so. Tonight, full moon through the haze, storm watch up. By bedtime, fine mist of snow in the wind.

2004: A bright sunny morning with light frost and all kinds of birds singing: starlings, chickadees, sparrows, doves, cardinals, crows. Squirrels are chasing each other through the locust and Osage trees. Clouds moved in throughout the afternoon, and when Jeanie and I went to bed at about 9:00 this evening, a storm moved across Yellow Springs with booming thunder and lightning – the only thunderstorm on January 1st in the past quarter of a century.

2005: Cardinals began singing in the fog this morning at 7:40. They continued off and on for almost half an hour as though it were the 1st of February instead of the New Year's Day. And a sign of good luck for 2005: A camelback cricket in the bathtub when I went to take a shower.

2006: South Glen: The river was high and fast, dull gray and green. October and November leaves had become part of my pathways, worn into the new mud. Some moss was growing on rotting logs. Coralberries and black privet berries were till holding. Chickweed and garlic mustard were spreading slowly across the forest floor. The hulls of last June's sweet rockets and August's wild cucumbers were empty, brittle and delicate like shed snakeskin. The Japanese knotweed leaves were hanging like huge russet cocoons. Milkweed pods were stained and empty. Osage fruit was darkening quickly, breaking down, squashy.

      Taking my time, I checked the buds on trees and shrubs: Hard, scarlet buds on the wild multiflora roses; box elder buds, barely visible, tucked tightly to their green branches; privet buds, minute and black; pale, supple buds of the honeysuckle; on the blackberry canes were blood-red buds, their color spreading to the sides of the stalks.

I felt the fleshy, orange buds of the buckeyes; the tight, round, silver buds of the dogwoods, each one marking the tip of its branch; the stiff, woody buds of the crab apples; the pale green buds of the lilac; the sharp and thorn-like buds of the American beech; the deep purple bud clusters of the red maples; the phallic protrusions of the ginkgo.

I measured the gray velvety buds of the white magnolia; the tiny russet linden buds; the yellow-brown, fat sweet gum buds growing beside their dangling fruit; birch buds with their willowy catkins; the buds of the tree-of-heaven, hiding in the hollows of last year's branches; flushed azalea buds protected by their shining leaves.

2008: Sun and a light wind, morning temperature in the 20s. I heard a robin peeping in the bushes as I fed the sparrows.

2010: After a foggy New Year's Eve that shut down the Columbus airport in the afternoon, today was cold and partly cloudy, and Neysa's plane took off for Miami Beach on time. Long flocks of geese heading south over the freeway as we drove back to Yellow Springs.

2011: Ruby Nicholson reported a kettle of 49 buzzards today, "all in one pine tree on President Street."

2012: Bluebirds reported in the Glen today, the same day I saw them in 1988: an overwintering flock or an early return? At our feeders in the yard: a downy woodpecker, a red-bellied woodpecker, tufted titmice, chickadees, cardinals and sparrows. When I walked Bella this morning, I found a violet periwinkle in bloom by the sidewalk. Coming back from church, I saw a robin scavenging for worms by the side of the street.

2013: Goshen, Indiana: On the trip north from Yellow Springs, snow on the land throughout, we saw only two murmurations of starlings, but when I went out to walk Bella well after dark, I heard sandhill cranes going over town, chattering and squawking, heading southwest, high above me.

2014: Crows came through at 7:47 this morning. Walking Bella at 9:30, I heard robins (and saw two in the bushes), whistling starlings, sparrows, a cardinal, a tufted titmouse, a nuthatch and a red-bellied woodpecker. Mild in the 40s today, storm forecast for tonight. Around 3:20 in the afternoon, I took Bella out to Ellis Pond. As we began to walk, I thought I heard sandhill cranes. I looked up but couldn't see anything, walked over towards where I thought the sound was coming from, but still couldn't see cranes. And then the calls stopped.

But when I got home, I had a phone message from Michele at the Tecumseh Land Trust. She reported a flock of sandhills over the pond there at about 3:00 p.m., possibly the same birds that I tried to find.

A call and note from John filled out details of the sandhills' visit to the sky over Yellow Springs:

"Sometime after 3:00, I heard the sound," he wrote. "I ran inside and called my mom and said they were passing to the east— I couldn't see them. I went back outside and still heard them, but was disoriented.

"Finally out in the intersection of Winter and Union Streets, I saw the flock: 71 (we counted them from Jane's photos). My neighbor, Laura, was walking her dog. 'Do you hear them? It's the cranes!' she said.

"We watched the flock for a good ten minutes, roughly over DeWine's Pond. A small crowd formed in the street. My mom was also engaging passersby on her street to behold their passing. She said two had gone over very low just after I had called.

"After the main flock climbed several hundred feet, to maybe a thousand feet, they headed off to the southwest. Interestingly, while they were circling, they were very chatty, as if checking in, commenting on their progress; but they really quieted down after they resumed their migration. My neighbor also noted this behavior."

And John closed with an original haiku:

John Blakelock, "New Year's Cranes"

2016: Dianne reports a vast flock of robins in the trees around her mother's nursing facility this afternoon. "There were so many I thought they were starlings," she said.

2017: Jill heard robins in the neighborhood and cranes flying over today.

2018: Deep record cold throughout the eastern half of the country, freezing far down to the Gulf. Low last night was -7 degrees officially, but my phone said -13 at 3:30 in the morning. Tonight, the full moon at perigee, "supermoon." Tomorrow night is expected to break the record of 1887. Casey reports seeing a bald eagle near Ellis Pond this week.

2023: Two brief outings this morning: Crows at 7:40 and a formation of maybe two dozen geese flew low over High Street.

Sam Hamill, "Two Songs for Tanabata Matsuri"

January 2nd
The 2nd Day of the Year

*I love the winter, with its imprisonment and its cold, for it compels
the prisoner to try new fields and resources.*

Henry David Thoreau

Sunrise/set: 7:57/5:21
Day's Length: 9 hours 24 minutes
Average High/Low: 35/20
Average Temperature: 28
Record High: 61 - 1916
Record Low: - 6 – 1887/-11 – 2018

The Daily Weather
There is a ten percent chance of a high in the 50s or 60s
today. Most of the afternoons, however, are cooler: ten percent of
them are in the 40s, sixty-five percent in the 30s, ten percent in the
20s, five in the single digits. Precipitation occurs six years in ten.
Cloudy days outnumber sunny days by three to one. There is a five
percent chance of the morning to be below zero.

The Natural Calendar:
A Rough Timetable
for the Calls of Yellow Springs Crows
*Early this morning crows flew westward over the prairie, cawing
in the fresh, temperate air, their voices as always filling the
morning with the promise of spring.*

August Derleth, *A Countryman's Journal*

Among the most consistent morning companions to residents
of Yellow Springs are its crows. They leave their roosts and call
about 15 to 20 minutes before sunrise throughout the year, and are
especially welcome between September and January, when most
other birds have either stopped singing or have left for the South.

In something of the same way that bells on churches or
public buildings announce the passage of the hours, the crows call

out the passage of the year. When the village is coldest, the crows usually awaken between 7:30 and 8:00 a.m., depending on temperature, cloud cover and precipitation. As the sun begins to rise earlier, however, they follow a more rigorous timetable a little like the one given below (in Eastern Standard Time). No matter what the actual sunrise time, the interval between daybreak and the crows' rough song will be similar to the following:

Date	Sunrise	Crow Calls
January 1	7:57	7:45
February 1	7:44	7:20
March 1	7:09	6:50
April 1	6:20	6:00
May 1	5:36	5:15
June 1	5:09	4:50
July 1	5:10	4:55
August 1	5:33	5:15
September 1	6:02	5:45
October 1	6:31	6:16
November 1	7:04	6:50
December 1	7:37	7:25

Daybook

1984: Beets dug after brief thaw. They were soft, ruined by the hard freeze.

1985: To Virginia: Blackbirds flocking in the mountains. Buzzards circling near Arlington. The vultures disappear from Yellow Springs at the end of October, but they do not winter so far south as I thought.

1988: Geese fly over 11:12 a.m. Sycamore Hole had a thin layer of ice, but the ice on the inlet that come from the old mill was so thick I could walk across on it, a few feet from my best fishing spot.

1989: A long walk in middle prairie at South Glen, listening to the wind in the trees. It sounded to me as if an ocean were on the other side of the hills, waves from an aerial tide. At home, almost a hundred birds at the feeder by Neysa's window, sparrows and starlings. Their numbers and their bantering broke the depression that had come over me earlier in the day.

1990: South Glen: At Sycamore Hole, ice nine or ten inches thick has been pushed up on shore by the thaw, the first time ice so thick since the Decembers of '78 and '83. Portions of the river are open, others cluttered with slabs of broken ice. Along the paths, the winter plants are strong, just like in the garden at home, as though the December freeze had never come.

1992: Two more hyacinths push up in the warm winter. First mother-of-millions blooms in the greenhouse. No trace of the cold of 1989 and 1990.

1993: First crocus foliage seen in the front garden; the leaves emerge despite the relatively severe December. One pale forsythia flower has come out on the east hedge.

1994: Four flocks of geese seen over the freeway at noon, and another came over Yellow Springs near four this afternoon. Robins are appearing throughout the village, probably wintering over and getting hungry, having used up all the food in the woods.

1999: Wind steady this morning with the first blizzard in four years. The snow is maybe three or four inches deep and drifting. The whistling wind is surging and tossing up snow like surf. By afternoon, the barometer is down to 29.65, snow and sleet done, the air relatively quiet, the sky covered by low gray stratus clouds.

2000: The crows were late this morning: 7:50. Cardinal at 8:24; seems like I haven't heard their full song for a month or so.

2006: Coming back from a bike ride along the pathway north late this warm afternoon, I was intercepted by a thunderstorm, hail and rain, the sun glowing through a peach-colored bank of altostratus, dove-gray above and below.

2008: Six inches of snow overnight, tufts of white on the rose of Sharon bushes. Most schools closed. The sparrows work to find a few seeds at the empty bird feeder, but no crows or starlings heard this morning. The wind is still blowing, sky gray, snow still drifting.

2009: A soft morning in the 20s with sun and the call of crows. When the clouds are gone, the dawn twilight is so strong a full hour before sunrise. Altostratus clouds in the afternoon, high in the 40s, the atmosphere quiet as if waiting for the wind to shift to the west and north.

2012: Light snow and wind throughout the day. Great variety of birds at the feeder yesterday and today: a wren, the first juncos in weeks, a starling, three doves, many cardinals, titmice, chickadees, sparrows, a downy, a red-bellied woodpecker, and a nuthatch. And at a little after 2:00 in the afternoon, Jeanie heard something that sounded a little like bamboo scraping on our windows. But it was too loud to be the bamboo. I thought maybe the teapot was making strange noises. About fifteen minutes later, Suzanne Patterson, so excited and happy, called from the Dharma Center to say she had seen about sixty sand hill cranes flying over heading southwest. Then John Blakelock called to report the same flock coming from the east, flying low. "They were so low," he said, "they were in trouble!" So the noise we heard was the cranes coming down High Street.

John's note came a little later: "Hey Bill - Was amazed to hear a large flock of cranes come over right around two this afternoon. They came out of the west, and were very low, just above the treetops. They were fluting in a plaintive fashion and struggling, really getting pushed around by the wind and snow and flapping much more than when they have a better altitude and a decent tailwind. By the time I got outside they were partially obscured by the Jail House, but I could see around 25 to 30. They had begun to climb and were back on a southbound course. I was worried about them. The mild December apparently seduced them into staying later than normal up at Pulaski, Indiana. Then this storm and the first significant lake-effect snow of the season made them realize they needed to bug out, NOW! I think they might take bearings from the patterned shingle designs I put on my roof."

2014: Several inches of snow overnight, and deep cold forecast for the week ahead, yesterday's sandhills flying before the storm. Cardinal in the distance at 9:45 this morning.

2018: Record cold this morning at minus 11 in Dayton. In Cedarville, Jeff had minus 13. Freezing temperatures far into the Deep South. Starlings drinking at the waterfall of the open pond. In spite of the long cold spell, Jeff said he had dug down under his compost pile, and the dirt had not frozen at all.

2020: Ed Oxley reports that his snowdrops were in bloom this morning.

2021: A cloudy and mild beginning to 2021. One of the hellebores in the dooryard garden is budded – after a December four degrees above normal. I thought I heard sandhills after lunch, but it was just a murder of crows excited about a hawk.

2022: Cloudy, rainy and mild the first two days of the year. At least 400 Canadian geese estimated overwintering at Ellis Pond.

2023: John and Lisa report seeing about a dozen sandhill cranes over Belmont Park in Dayton.

The evening was clear, no clouds or wind.... Moon three quarters full rising over the eastern ridge. I could be happy enough just observing this, day after day....

Harlan Hubbard

I sing the cycle of my country's year,
I sing the tillage, and the reaping sing

Vita Sackville-West.

Sunrise/set: 7:57/5:22
Day's Length: 9 hours 25 minutes
Average High/Low: 35/20
Average Temperature: 28
Record High: 65 – 1897, 62 – 2023
Record Low: - 17 – 1904

The Daily Weather

January 3rd brings a five percent chance of a high in the 50s , a 25 percent chance of 40s, a 50 percent chance of 30s, a ten percent chance of 20s and a ten percent chance of highs just in the teens. Precipitation occurs 50 percent of the time, and clouds dominate 60 percent of the days. Five percent of the morning temperatures fall below zero.

The Natural Calendar

In some ways, nothing has changed with the arrival of the New Year. The trees are still bare, and no new sprouts have appeared in the undergrowth. Most pussy willow catkins are thin and tight. Forsythia buds show no hint of their February blush. Last year's plants, however, are giving way to the weather, leading the landscape back toward the sun.

January scatters the last of the wildflowers, or it feeds them to the sparrows and downy woodpeckers. Almost all the goldenrod and aster seeds are gone. Only a few wingstem and ironweed kernels still hang to their stalks. The hulls of last June's sweet rockets and August's wild cucumbers are empty, brittle and delicate like shed snakeskin. The Japanese knotweed leaves hang like huge russet cocoons. Milkweed pods are stained and empty.

Almost all of Early Winter's honeysuckle berries have been eaten by birds or have fallen in the wind by now, and foliage of

Japanese knotweed and oakleaf hydrangea is finally ceding to the cold. The dried flower clusters of purple coneflowers and zinnias, tough and unyielding a month ago, crumble between your fingers. Honeysuckle and euonymus berries still hang to their branches, but their firmness is gone. Osage fruit is darkening quickly, breaking down, becoming squashy.

The Sun

Perihelion, the point at which the Earth and the Sun are closest to one another, occurs in the first week of the month. Even though the new year's sunlight is more intense than the sunlight of aphelion (which occurs in July), the day across the North is almost six hours shorter in January than it is in midsummer.

Across the South, sunrise remains close to 7:00 a.m. throughout January, but the day's length increases by more than 20 minutes this month, as sunset becomes later 40 seconds or so each evening. In the North, the sun's morning movement is a little more obvious, sunrise becoming earlier by between 15 and 20 minutes. It is sunset time, however, which makes the biggest difference in the day's length, becoming later by up to 40 minutes. In all, up to an hour can be subtracted from the night by the end of January, depending on one's location in the northern tier of states. And from January 3 forward, night along the 40th Parallel contracts by at least one minute every 24 hours until June.

The Shooting Stars

The Quadrantid meteors reach their peak after midnight near this date.

Daybook

1987: The excitement of the daybook has been a simple one. I see a parallel to my own seeming lack of growth and change. I see that nature is as deliberate as I am, and that the movements I make in a day toward my purposes are as slow as the progress of a season. So, I think, my seasons might, in time, take on the bright color, the clear direction, the sense, and the harmony of the year.

1998: Henry Meyer called up this afternoon. Ladybugs are coming out around his house, maybe a dozen or so every warm afternoon.

His neighbor has them, too. Doug Hinkley says the Champneys also have the winter ladybugs. Seems they are the Asian lady bugs introduced a decade or so in New Orleans, and they have spread north with a vengeance. Henry says that they have even dive-bombed the Community Chorus when they were practicing up at the high school.

1999: Rain last night, turning the ground snow to slush, streets slippery when I went out walking, no cars at all. Today, the wind is back, the water on the streets frozen, pond nearly closed with ice. A song sparrow and a cardinal feeding at the south garden feeder at 8:00 this morning.

2004: A large flock of geese flew over this morning about 7:50. They were loud and heading south. A few minutes later, they were back, going north. Through the afternoon, heavy rains filled the yard with water.

2008: No cowbirds or woodpeckers or starlings so far this winter at the east garden feeders. No finches at the finch feeder, only an occasional cardinal and chickadee at the bedroom feeder.

2009: A mild day, sun in the morning, pastel clouds in the afternoon, rain for tonight. Only sparrows at the feeder, one robin called at dawn. Around noon, a squirrel was screeching in the back locust trees.

2010: Bitter cold but sunny. Jeanie heard a titmouse before 8:00. Geese were honking west of town about 10:30. Neysa reports unusually cold weather in Miami Beach, Florida, highs only in the 40s.

2011: The coldest morning of the year, the clouds breaking up and the wind holding steady. At 11:20, Jenny Copperwaite called with a report of sandhill cranes, about twenty, she thought, heading south. Then Lauren Heaton called, had seen what she thought was a very big flock, and then Kitty Jensen called. She had been out in the South Glen along the river with Kumar when a flock of maybe thirty came over. I was downtown around that time, but I didn't hear them. Jeanie, at home, did hear them, though.

2012: I check the oak leaf hydrangea by the back porch. It often keeps half its leaves, even when the days stay below freezing. I stand and look at the woodpile for a while, trying to estimate how much wood is left. I look in the front garden to see if the snowdrops have come up; usually they have, at least a little, their white tips an easy gauge of earliest spring - that is unless they are covered with snow.

I check the pussy willow catkins; sometimes I count how many are opening. That's another way to measure the progress of the year. I take a look at the honeysuckle bushes, note whether any of their berries are left. I finger the seed heads of the New England asters to see if all the seeds are gone. I kick the fat Osage fruits to understand how they are doing: they are chartreuse green when they tumble down in October and November, turn yellower and yellower through the fall, start to get mushy in the middle of winter, fall apart in spring.

I find the plants that keep their green through the coldest times: the hellebores, the creeping charley, the chickweed and pachysandra, garlic mustard, mullein, sweet rocket, and sweet William, and I am reassured by their deep color and hardiness. I look under the mulch to see if the peony stalks have started to come up. I bend down and scratch the dirt in the rhubarb patch; sometime the first red knuckles of next year's pies are visible.

2015: At just a couple minutes before ten this morning, a great flock of starlings came from the east and settled in the back trees, from the south Osage into the locusts and the white mulberry on the west and the hackberry to the north. They chattered and clucked until 10:05 and the a loud car passing by spooked them and the whole flock lifted up and flew away to the northwest.

2016: John Blakelock called at 1:30 this afternoon: He had heard sandhill cranes heading south over his house – said that his friend Laura had seen them in Fairborn around noon). Later in the afternoon, Sue Gilkey reported that she and her husband saw 44 sandhills flying over Wilberforce-Clifton Road and Cedarville-Yellow Springs Road at about 3:45. A little later still, Paul Van

Ausdale called: His wife, Carol, counted 102 sandhills above South Glen about the same time as Sue saw her pod. Paul added that he had found the vernal witch-hazel at the Ellis Pond arboretum in full flower.

2017: Ed Oxley has the first snowdrop in bloom.

2018: Winter Storm Grayson spreads ice and snow from central Florida north all along the East Coast. Deep cold continues to keep lows near or below zero in the northern half of the United States, hard freeze warnings far into the Carolinas and Georgia. We cancelled our drive to Florida for tomorrow, blocked by dangerous road conditions through the mountains down past Jacksonville, Florida.

2019: Once again (like in 2017), Ed Oxley has snowdrops blooming the morning of January 3rd. He had one flowering on December 1 back in 2011, December 15th in 2015.

2022: Casey reports a flock of black buzzards near his property.

2023: Warm and misty, 62 degrees. I stacked wood in the rain. When I checked Ellis Pond today: No geese. But when I came out of the post office, five formations flew over, maybe 150 - 200 birds in all. Winter storm moving east from the Plains today.

Changes in the weather transform the very feel of the world's presence, altering the medium of awareness in a manner that affects every breathing being in our vicinity. We sometimes refer to such weather phenomena, taken together, as "the elements," a phrase that suggests how basic, how primary, these powers are to the human organism.

David Abram, *Becoming Animal, An Earthly Cosmology*

January 4th
The 4th Day of the Year

Chill airs and wintry winds! My ear
Has grown familiar with your song;
I hear it in the opening year,
I listen, and it cheers me long.

Henry Wadsworth Longfellow

Sunrise/set: 7:57/5:23
Day's Length: 9 hours 26 minutes
Average High/Low: 35/20
Average Temperature: 27
Record High: 63 – 1897
Record Low: - 18 – 1904

The Daily Weather
There is a ten percent chance of a warm afternoon in the 60s today, and another ten percent of 50s. Highs in the 40s come ten percent of the time, 30s come 35 percent, 20s twenty-five percent, teens five percent and single digits five percent. The sun appears five days in ten. Rain falls 25 percent of the days, snow 15 percent. The relatively high likelihood for milder conditions can bring stiff south winds and even an occasional thunderstorm.

Natural Calendar
On bright sunny mornings, starlings, chickadees, pileated woodpeckers, sparrows and crows may be calling. Overwintering robins look for the last honeysuckle berries. Multicolored Asian lady beetles, late autumn migrants, could be emerging on windowsills on warm afternoons. Owls are staking out their territories in the woods.

During warmer Northern winters and across the South, fresh foliage of columbine, dandelion, garlic mustard, sedum, wild onion, ground ivy, leafcup and celandine appears in sheltered areas. Skunk cabbage, dock and ragwort rise in the swamps. Watercress is bright green in the streams. New mint grows back under the protection of a southern wall.

In the pastures, spring thistles, sweet rockets, and great mullein add basil leaves when the weather is temperate. Parsley and kale could be holding out in the garden. Three inches below the mulch, blanched daffodils are pushing up.

Daybook

1989: A cardinal singing this morning, 8:40, sunny, 15 degrees.

1991: The sun is in and out over the river this afternoon. The water shines with ripples and small, brisk waves, silver, then momentary blues, then grays. The oaks are black against the last of the snow. The colors around me deepen, lighten depending on the thickness of the clouds and the remnants of fog from one path to the next. The wind doesn't reach here into middle prairie, but I can hear it coming up from the south.

An Osage hillside: the yellow wood glows like the flush of expanding spring buds. Below the Osage, hardy green chickweed and wild onion, garlic mustard, purple deadnettle, hemlock. The rain brings them to life, deepening and enriching. The ground is sown with their pointers and dials that prove there is enough time. The new year will never be longer, will never be slower or simpler. I have counted everything before; I know how many days are left, how many days until I can see whatever piece of spring I want.

From the top of the ridge, the river is a path of light. As I walk down and around a sycamore, a sudden patch of fog blurs the divisions between the hills, and the bright curves of the rivern disappear. The enclosure of whiteness shows both the confinement and the freedom of the valley. In the fog, there is no other side to the Little Miami. I have no landmarks, no limits.

1992: Morning sky with openings of gold in the east against creamy gray, long bars of clouds. Some hyacinths up an inch in the south garden, some crocus three inches. There's a new leaf on one forsythia branch, and on the clematis. All day rain, high reached 59, but no worms seen on the sidewalks; they know it's winter.

1994: Half a dozen robins in the ginkgo tree outside my window all day long in spite of the wind and snow.

1998: Warm into the lower 60s today, mostly cloudy, but a little sun now and then. The cardinals sang all morning, the starlings were cackling as I walked home from church, and now the sparrows are chattering through the afternoon. Four woodpeckers working the back trees. I saw a chickadee passing through the apple tree. The pond temperature has risen to 50 degrees, up a full ten degrees from last week and the Christmas cold front.

At the Covered Bridge with Buttercup and Gus, the bulldogs: late afternoon, and the clouds suddenly clearing, the ground wet and soft, smelling faintly of spring, river gurgling, sun setting through cirrus giving a ruddy tint to the pale sycamore bark and to the shells of late summer wildflowers, the Japanese knotweed leaves hanging like huge russet cocoons, the red and purple stems of the raspberries, the goldenrod and ironweed and aster seeds white as frost.

1999: Deep cold today, the high getting up just to 15 degrees, and below-zero temperatures forecast for tonight. The pond is frozen over except for a small hole where the heater floats. All the ground is covered with half a foot or more of snow. Real winter for a change. And another major storm is forecast for the 10th.

2002: Several cardinals were singing as I rode my bike down High Street to Susi's at 8:25 this morning. Titmouse heard yesterday or the day before. No blue jays heard yet this winter.

2004: The heavy rains continue, more of the yard under water than I've ever seen it. The pond is full to overflowing, the first time that has ever happened. The airport says only an inch of rain has fallen, but I estimate four to six inches here. Yellow Springs Creek and the Little Miami are far over their banks, spreading throughout the bottomland.

2005: In Goshen, Judy thinks that she is seeing goldfinches turning gold. Is it the sunlight or a dramatic shift in climate?

2007: Greg called to report seeing the pileated woodpecker at his suet feeder for the first time (earlier than usual, he thinks). Throughout the East, the warm January is producing very tangible effects: trees in flower at the Brooklyn arboretum and throughout Washington D.C. Many bulbs are in blooming in the nation's capital, pictures of iris featured on the news. At home, daylily foliage is coming up in front of Don's house.

2008: South wind blowing this morning, snow and ice thumping down from the east roof of the old part of our house, thaw underway.

2009: A soft, foggy morning. When I went outside near dawn, I could hear the chirping chattering of what sounded like a flock of starlings far beyond the west end of town.

2010: Casey called this morning with a report of four buzzards in the woods. He added that the owls on his place were "carrying on" around New Year's Eve. Then at about 2:00, Casey called again: "Get in your pickup," he said, "and drive down Grinnell Road by the spring. There's a deer carcass there and about fifteen buzzards." I did what he said to do, and indeed there were fifteen *black* buzzards (not the normal turkey vultures), tame as could be, feeding by the side of the road. And Jerry Rohrs reported from Archbold, in northern Ohio: "A reader just stopped in to report 'hundreds' of fat robins gathered at the local cemetery. Are they going to a funeral? Or are they gathering to begin their migration? Or have they missed that and are now stuck here for the winter?

2011: This morning, crows called at the earliest time so far in the winter: 7:33 a.m. Coming home from Xenia, we saw the flock of black buzzards eating something near the herb store.

2012: Birds fed heavily today, and the first flock of starlings came down from the woods to eat suet and to compete with the sparrows on the ground.

2013: A young cardinal is singing whenever I come out into the yard, morning or afternoon.

2014: Starlings are flocking in small groups around the neighborhood, the first time I've seen them here together in such numbers this winter.

2015: One large murmuration of starlings seen as I came back from Kettering this noon. Yesterday's mild temperatures and hard rain are ceding to steady wind from the west and the deepest cold of the winter so far. In the back yard, after a mild winter, a little more than four degrees above normal, the chickweed, henbit, bittercress and lamium have all spread widely throughout the garden. At the west border, euonymus berries are falling. Maybe the starlings scattered them the other day. Maybe they brought the starlings.

2017: I looked out of Jill's living room window and saw the lawn all white. The first snow of the winter had come overnight. Yesterday's sandhill cranes flew before the cold, forecasting. And then Bob Huston called today: he had just seen them, sun shining on their feathers, heading south, and he counted 36.

2021: Ed Oxley reports snowdrops blooming.

2022: Robins peeping throughout the neighborhood this morning. No starlings in town yet this winter.

2023: Several hundred geese in the fields at Ellis Pond. During the last three days of the thaw, some movement toward Spring. In my dooryard, three Lenten roses have produced large white buds, and thin spears of snowdrops have pushed up around the euonymus vines. No robins heard in the neighborhood lately.

There is no season such delight can bring,
As summer, autumn, winter, and the spring.

William Browne

January 5th
The 5th Day of the Year

The good observer of nature exists in fragments, a trait here and a trait there. Each person sees what it concerns him to see.

John Burroughs

Sunrise/set: 7:57/5:24
Day's Length: 9 hours 27 minutes
Average High/Low: 35/20
Average Temperature: 27
Record High: 62 – 1939
Record Low: - 22 – 1884

The Daily Weather

Today is often windy and brisk due to the arrival of the month's second cold front. Ten percent of the highs are only in the teens or below; 20s occur a fourth of the time, 30s on 45 percent of the afternoons, 40s on 15 percent, 50s on five percent. Lows drop below zero 15 percent of all January 5ths, presaging some of the deepest cold of the year. Skies are totally overcast five days in ten, and precipitation occurs close to 40 percent of the years.

Natural Calendar

The Big Dipper's Merak and Dubhe, pointers for the North Star, are now positioned east-west after dark, marking the midpoint of the calendar year. From that center, I can survey the land and seasons all around my yard in southwestern Ohio. Knowing the average temperatures here, I can gauge the weather anywhere in the eastern half of the country. If I walk east or west from town along the axis of Merak and Dubhe, five hundred miles in each direction, the averages hold to those in my village, dipping slightly in the mountains, rising near the coast. Following Polaris north, I find the world becomes colder by one degree every twenty-five miles. When I go south, guiding on the Dog Star, Sirius, the weather warms by one degree every twenty-five miles all the way to the Gulf of Mexico.

A provincial season, closely observed, is a map to other

distant seasons. If I set my watch by the bloodroot in the back woods, that time, with a weather graph or two, will be good enough to make a calendar of bloodroot in a thousand counties. From within the landmarks in this middle kingdom, the outlying areas come into perspective. When I travel through the country in the summer, the canon of local flora serves me well. I can guide on Queen Anne's lace, milkweed, birdsfoot trefoil, and chicory all the way to northern Minnesota, east to Washington D.C., west past St. Louis, and south into Georgia. The flowers keep me grounded to Yellow Springs as well as mark my way.

And when winter becomes too long, I retreat to my charts. They tell me that between the middle of January through the middle of May, spring moves from New Orleans at a rate of six miles per day or one degree every four days. The seasons are variable and unpredictable, but those average rates of vernal progress hold. Whatever is lost with one cold wave is gained in a later thaw. When Merak and Dubhe have rotated ninety degrees, pointing north-south instead of east-west, it will be Middle Spring. Hepatica will be old in Tennessee, barely opening in Michigan, full bloom in the middle of Ohio and Indiana.

Daybook

1984: Even after two weeks of very cold weather, the leafcup and sweet rocket foliage is vigorous. Garlic mustard, though, is drooping.

1985: Geese fly over at sundown.

1988: Freezing weather deepens, but a cardinal sings at eight o'clock this morning.

1991: Bursts of sparrow chatter, loud and excited. When does it become spring chatter, charged with territory and mating?

1993: The month began cold, turned warm; this Ohio winter is so soft. I look from my office window at the mulched trees, black mounds of shredded bark around them, underlining them, accenting their dark trunks, drawing them cleanly against the pale green lawn, the orange brick buildings, the gray, low sky.

1994: Long line of geese seen from my window at work today. As on January 2nd, they are restless before the storm moving in.

1997: This morning, a cardinal sang at 8:05, and crows passed through earlier. This afternoon, I walked at the mill, temperature in the upper 50s, light rain. Signs of beavers at work, several small saplings chewed off. Chickadees chattering, a pileated woodpecker calling in the distance.

2002: When I walked out to get firewood at 8:00 this morning: one cardinal was singing, and then a titmouse called.

2004: A few daffodils are pushing up along the front walk, almost covered by the recent flooding.

2005: Steady rains have flooded the yard, covering almost a fourth of its surface, completely submerging the sidewalk from the porch to the street. Cardinals still sing on and off.

2007: Heavy rain today repeated the yard flooding of this same day in 2005. In fact, the yard has been flooding almost once a week, the ground apparently saturated. Screech owl heard as I returned from a walk with Bella this evening about 9:00 o'clock.

2009: The first tufted titmouse call heard this morning around 9:30, and then a cardinal. When I walked Bella a little later, robins were chirping near Limestone Street, and there was a twittering of birds throughout the neighborhood.

2010: No crows heard this morning. Starlings were bunching in Moya's trees when I came back from TK's around 10:30.

2012: Crows around 7:30 this morning, sun and 25 degrees. Mild in the 40s this afternoon, but the Dakotas, the Plains and northern Minnesota had record high temperatures with no change in sight.

2013: Crows late this morning, 7:55.

2014: Mild in the 30s this morning, cold wave due tonight. Crows at 7:44, cardinals off and on in the morning.

2017: Deep cold continues throughout the Northeast and Southeast, Jill's friend, Ann, stranded in Charleston, South Carolina, in six inches of snow, freezing temperatures into northern Florida, parts of Boston flooded by tidal surge and wind. Here on High Street, starlings cluster and flutter around Moya's side yard and in the street. Liz writes: "Lots of crows in the neighborhood today! Stunning against the white snow."

2019: In the dooryard, snowdrops are a few inches high under the month, and a few crocus spears have appeared. In the circle garden, a couple of hyacinths are just coming out. All around the neighborhood, henbit is growing stronger.

And Emily writes: 'Today I am hearing new sounds of the season! The chickadees, black–capped, are singing their "Spring is here!" song. First time I've heard that since summer. The nuthatches were very vociferous and a bowl today, too. I heard a laughing song that was new for them this season. Mating song? And the titmice were singing. And the house finches are singing. It's quite a sing-songy day! Feels like spring from the birds and the sun."

2021: Every morning, I see the old mock orange bush on the east side of the building. Every year, I see it leaf out in late March or early April, and the first fully-formed leaf is always a milestone in my year. Today I noticed that the very last leaf had fallen, opening the way for spring.

Journal

The morning before New Year's Eve, the sun was warm, and I took a walk in the bottomland along the river. The further I walked, the more I noticed the moss around me, and I realized that almost all the stones were green, that the fallen logs were green, that the rotting stumps were green, that the oldest trees overhanging the river were covered with the thickest, most luxurious green moss, fat and bushy, an inch thick in places. Dry streambeds were filled with green rocks and branches. Limestone boulders were bearded with moss, speckled with sedum and lichens. Everywhere I looked I found islands of summer among the dead leaves, and they drew my vision through vertical pillars of green up into the blue sky.

This winter, I have been reading essays by Thomas Merton and St. Bernard. Both of these authors obsessively extract novel interpretations of events in the Christian liturgical year. St. Bernard is especially gifted of at enumerating things such as the three aspects of Advent or the twelve rungs on the ladder of humility. In his lists, he explored many unlikely dimensions of his topic, often reaching well beyond the expected to achieve his desired number of insights.

As I walked, I wondered what Bernard would do with all these green Scriptures that grew silently around me. He was a man who made tiers of everything, filled in the empty spaces of events, created sequences out of concepts, found allegory wherever he looked. I imagined him without his Jesus and without his Church, helping me to see what really lay before me. I imagined him building the green ladder of this day, finding four transcendent stages in deep winter, six hidden levels in the thickness of mosses, nine miraculous shades of January jade, twelve secret dimensions of the living stones nestled among decaying leaves, fifteen lessons in the enigmatic deer paths that cut carpets of bright chickweed into geometric icons, twenty symbols of inner life growing from the ancient tree stumps, thirty signs of resurrection in the crossed branches of the hoary sycamores, all the meanings I would ever need flowering from Gaia's Word.

After a cold December,
I went out through town
To the headwaters of spring,
To the watershed of time,
Touching buds in the thaw.

Leon Quel

January 6th
The 6th Day of the Year

Perceiv'st thou not the process of the year,
How the four seasons in four forms appear,
Resembling human life in ev'ry shape they wear?

Ovid (tr. Garth)

Sunrise/set: 7:57/5:25
Day's Length: 9 hours 28 minutes
Average High/Low: 35/20
Average Temperature: 27
Record High: 66 – 1946
Record Low: - 22 – 1884

The Daily Weather

The 6th is cloudy two thirds of the time, brings rain or snow 25 percent of the time, warms to the 50s five percent of the time, brings 40s on a fourth of the days, 30s on 40 percent of the days, 20s twenty-five percent of the time, and teens five percent of the time. Below-zero mornings occur only once or twice in a quarter century.

Natural Calendar

Observe the daily circle of the sun,
And the short year of each revolving moon:
By them thou shalt foresee the following day,
Nor shall a starry night thy hopes betray.

Poor Richard's Almanack, 1733

In milder winters, snowdrops are often showing by this date. Back in the first half January of 1992, a friend of mine called with just such news.

"They're not only up," Janet said, "they're almost budding, you know how they do, the white petals just kind of peeking out!" She had three hyacinths coming up too, each an inch tall, underneath her bird feeder, "and there's even a tulip and a daffodil!"

Lately, my snowdrop scout is Ed Oxley, who lives a little north of Yellow Springs. Even the chilling December of 2010 did not keep his flowers down, and he showed me photos of a November snowdrop, its petals fully emerged.

How often does it happen that bulbs are emerging at this time of year in Yellow Springs? It happened at least in 2020, 2015, 2014, 2013, 2012, 2009, 2008, 2007, 2004, 2000, 1990 and in 1989 (the temperature even approaching 60 during this week that year), and (based on December averages) in 1975, 1967, 1960, 1953, 1950, 1949 and so on during the more gentle Januarys back into history.

Daybook

1985: Bird feeding now well established in the back yard. Starlings and doves have joined the sparrows, finches and cardinals. Squirrels are regular visitors. Song sparrows come once in a while. A downy woodpecker explored the rotting Osage today. In the greenhouse, the marigolds are finished, impatiens weakened more and more by mealy bugs. Lettuce and first radishes are fully mature. Some geraniums are starting to recover from their December slump, more buds forming.

1991: Cardinal song strong at 8:10 a.m.

1992: Only a few honeysuckle berries seen today, and those were dark, hurt by the cold. They last through early winter, then deteriorate completely or are finished off by starlings and robins in January.

1994: A dozen robins in the grass at Wilberforce looking for fallen crab apples in the snow.

1999: The bitter cold lets up a little, but the barometer drops quickly, snow falling off and on, the wind increasing. In the greenhouse, mother-of-millions are starting to open. The winter tomatoes are in the middle of their best production ever; Neysa cut twenty or so the other day. There are dozens left. It's the February and March harvests that will be lean. Indoor chard continues to do well, but wilts easily with too much sun, and the older leaves are too tough to eat.

2005: After the melting of the 16-inch Christmas snowfall and the deluge, five inches of rain in the past few days, there is flooding everywhere. The Little Miami is way up over its banks, the water near the covered bridge reaching within maybe 50 feet of Grinnell Road. A repetition of last year's early January flooding, almost to the day.

2008: To Cincinnati in the thaw. Four flocks of geese seen flying over the freeway throughout the trip.

2010: Cardinal at 8:05 this morning. Jeff called before noon: He had just seen a flock of black buzzards was eating "something hairy" by the side of Grinnell Road. This afternoon from Vermont, Cathy writes about leaving food out for what she thinks is a vole in her house: "As for the vole, it's odd to feel connected to a little wild rodent in your house. When it doesn't show up I wonder if it's OK. When it makes loud rummaging noises at night, I get scared it has grown as large as a woodchuck. Sometimes it's very noisy and sometimes days go by with silence. But all the time, it eats what we put out and seems to like crackers and peanut butter and fresh apple slices the best. I thought it would like carrots since they're said to eat roots, but it left the carrots and removed the apples. Maybe it has a cache of dried apples by now, somewhere in our basement. Of course, I might also be feeding mice, who knows. Everyone but Charles thinks I'm nuts to feed it. I guess if I have a huge vole family come spring, I'll reconsider, but for now, I can't see putting it outside to freeze."

And Mary Sue sends this: "The two sandhill cranes are still here, settling into their roosting spot a little early this evening in the falling snow."

2012: Bella and I walked downtown in the warmth and sun. A few daffodils had pushed up in the southern exposures along Elm Street, and I saw a large black fly zooming around in front of a porch across from the church. Judy wrote from Goshen, Indiana: "Just a quick note to let you know - to paraphrase James Joyce -- a cardinal epiphanized this morning as Angel and I were walking. Earliest yet!" The high reached into the middle 50s this afternoon, March in January.

2014: Deep cold envelops the eastern half of the country, temperatures dropping steadily well below zero today, wind chills near 40 below. At the feeder, starlings have gathered to compete with the sparrows. Their appearance now is one of the earliest movements toward spring.

2017: In the middle of a deep cold wave, nighttime temperatures at zero, an ootheca of preying mantises hatched in Jill's dining room near the plants she brought in for the winter.

2018: Deep cold in Yellow Springs, below zero once again in the morning. And a crane sighting from Amy Crawford: "I saw 3 Sandhill cranes flying south over Yellow Springs-Fairfield Road near Carol Drive /east of Twin Towers park just before 3 pm on Saturday January 6."
      Jill and I drove south through West Virginia down to Charlotte, North Carolina, where temperatures were above freezing in the afternoon. No snow seen after we passed through the mountains and descended into Virginia. The rolling land was a soft dun color, like the fur coat of a sleeping winter beast. In Florida, news stories of iguanas falling out of trees from the cold (like Neysa reported from Miami Beach on the 7th of 2008).

2019: Sun and mild in the upper 40s. I heard a male cardinal sing and a female "chit" sound at 7:30 this morning. At the pond, a flock of about fifty geese floating. In the field across the way, another small flock hunkered down.

2021: Firm points of hyacinths pushing up just half an inch or so in the middle of the circle garden. And Emily Foubert wrote to say she heard a cardinal song from her sit spot. And John Blakelock saw a bald eagle: "This one was flying, about 150' up, heading South, between Snypp and Huston Roads. I was like, 'That is a BIG bird,' wondered if it might be a stray straggler sandhill crane for a sec. 'Not a blue heron.' Then it banked, and the afternoon sun caught its white tail, and then it cocked its head to the west, and I *saw the white head.* A few years back...2017, I saw one right where Snypp hits DYS, sitting atop a utility pole. Looking at the terrain, it could conceivably have a territory running along the Jacoby Valley. There are 3 good-sized farm ponds in the triangle between E. Hyde & Route 68, and a LOT of woods."

Journal

An epiphany is not a static or closed reality; it remains open. What is shown in one intense moment takes a long time to unfold.
Abbot E. D.

On Christmas morning, I got up about 5:00, went out into the greenhouse and listened to the wind and rain drive against the southeast corner of the house. I built up the fire in the wood stove and sat for almost an hour listening to the waves and eddies of the storm, the tin roof bucking and thumping against the rafters, the windows rattling, the leaky door of the stove moaning.

After an hour or so, the rain stopped, the gusts continuing for a while more, and then by sunrise, all was quiet. My yard lay in the windless center of a low-pressure cell, the sky clearing.

I went outside on the covered back porch to check the temperature: almost 50 degrees. Then I noticed a butterfly, a *polygonia comma*, perched on the head of the small stone crucifix one of my sisters had given the family some years ago. I conjectured that the insect might have been seduced by the warm south winds and had come out for spring; or maybe it had been driven from its winter quarters by the violence of the storm and had found refuge on the cross.

Now I am a wavering and superstitious Christian, easily swayed by signs and sacraments, and so the appearance of the *polygonia* on a crucifix in the wake of a freak rainstorm on Christmas morning was bound to trigger some uneasiness of spirit.

The nature of my discomfort was hard to name, and all kinds of associations passed through my mind for the next several days. The symbolism was obvious, of course, the butterfly that so many cultures associate with the soul - a creature of transformation, of rebirth, of metamorphosis - appearing so close to solstice, on the day commemorating the birth of the God who supposedly took on human form in the last of the darkest nights of the year. And if that were not enough, this winged visitor landed on the ultimate Christian icon!

But, at the same time, I knew that the *polygonia nativitatis* (as I named it) belonged to a hibernating species, and spent the winter here as an adult. It was, I reasoned, no great surprise that the unseasonable wind and the rain had forced it from its retreat. It was likely that innumerable butterflies had been swept out of their lairs and landed in improbable places that morning.

Still, I could not stop wanting this butterfly to mean something. Was it a messenger from my Irish Catholic ancestors? Was it one of those minute "butterfly effect" variables that might influence the entire weather of the world? Was this the butterfly whose wings would set off tsunamis and cyclones in the Indian Ocean? Was this butterfly actually the cause rather than the effect of the storm (as a Chaos Theory physicist might argue)? Was it an Isaiah of global warming?

The next morning at 7:00, I checked the crucifix: my butterfly was still there. The wind was shifting to the northwest, and the barometer was rising. The day remained mild, but then the temperature dropped to the 20s that night. On December 28, the high below freezing, the butterfly held to the cross all day.

Then when I went out to check it on the 29th, the temperature at 16 degrees, the *polygonia* was gone. I searched for it in the leaves below the cross, but it wasn't there. The encounter was over, and I was disappointed, having found only questions in my vigil.

A few days later, on Epiphany Sunday, I listened to Abbot Elias Dietz caution me to be patient: "An epiphany is not a static or closed reality; it remains open," he said. "What is shown in one intense moment takes a long time to unfold. No single manifestation, no single perceptible sign is capable of giving us faith or changing our hearts."

January 7th
The 7th Day of the Year

All things by immortal power near or far,
Hiddenly to each other linked are,
That thou canst not stir a flower
Without troubling a star.

Francis Thompson

Sunrise/set: 7:57/5:26
Day's Length: 9 hours 29 minutes
Average High/Low: 35/19
Average Temperature: 27
Record High: 66 – 2008
Record Low: - 12 – 1884

The Daily Weather

Today's temperature distribution: ten percent chance of highs in the 50s or 60s, fifteen percent of 40s, forty percent of 30s, twenty-five of 20s, and ten percent of teens. Rain is rare on this day, but snow falls 35 percent of the years. Below-zero temperatures almost never occur on the 7th.

Natural Calendar

Pussy Willow Cracking Season becomes apparent as occasional thaws pock Deep Winter, growing until pollen spreads across the fully emerged catkins in the early days of March. In milder years, the foliage of crocus, columbine, henbit, catnip, forget- me-not, garlic mustard, dandelion, wild onion, celandine, hemlock and ground ivy expands slowly between cold fronts, revealing the often-overlooked Season of Winter Leaves. January's second week moves the full Season of Winter Stars into the evenings. Orion lies in the center of the southern sky at 10:00 p.m. The Pleiades lead Taurus west; Gemini and Cancer follow in the east.

1988: Song sparrow seen, only an occasional visitor at the feeder, but more consistent than the juncos. The latter must have more problems with the house sparrow flock.

1989: Calm and mild all day, wind coming up at dusk. Cardinal singing across the butterfly preserve, then quiet up to the barn and back. Ground foliage bright and strong, one leafcup with a few small new leaves. At home, I was digging in the daffodil patch: two inches down, the yellow-headed sprouts were extending from their bulbs, well on the way to March. Geese flew over honking at 4:56 p.m.

1993: Heavy frost in the morning, then cirrus and altostratus throughout the day. Up to 40 this afternoon. Driving back from Wilberforce, I was accompanied by a housefly in the car trying to get out through the windshield. Where did it come from? Had it been roused from winter hibernation by the sun? Home from work: it seems the squirrels have learned to use their four-pronged corn wheel; a few kernels gone. It's taken them a week to figure it out.

1994: Covered Bridge habitat: Today a small flock of robins was feeding in the open mud at the swamp. Maybe half a dozen were under the ledge of the riverbank, flew across the water toward First Prairie when I walked over them.

2000: In the greenhouse, the whiteflies are getting stronger, the tomato plants stalky, the plants with the weakest soil base wilting in days of hard sun, recovering at night, but so vulnerable still. Every once in a while I hear a cardinal outside, clear and comforting.

2001: Smelled a skunk along Clifton Road this morning. Saw a flock of cardinals in the honeysuckle bushes.

2002: Robin eating berries from the hawthorn tree in front of the post office at 3:30 this afternoon.

2004: A silent flock of crows flies over at 7:45 a.m.

2005: A cardinal was singing at 7:40 when I went out to the back yard get wood this morning. Skies gray, the air damp, 27 degrees. In the greenhouse, the two coleus plants brought in from summer are getting pale, but they are still beautiful and healthy.

2008: A warm 60 degrees as I walked Bella in the alley this morning about 10:00. No birds singing, but the sparrows were waiting for their daily feeding in the bushes when I came home. At noon, the temperature was up to 66, surpassing the record high for today. I opened the front and back doors to let in the thaw. Neysa called from Miami Beach: it got so cold there, last week, she said, that a gecko sat on her hand to get warm, and that iguanas, unable to hold on because of the cold, fell out of trees on passers-by.

2009: Rain, sleet and snow this morning. Crows at 8:05. A squirrel calling in the back woods when I went out to get wood at 9:30. A cardinal sang about 10:00.

2012: Another sunny day with highs in the upper 40s, the winter exceptionally bright and warm so far this year. Crows were calling at 7:35 this morning - at least that early. Squirrels racing all around the back trees. Sparrows fed heavily, and the downy woodpecker came to the suet after they left.

2016: Sun and mild in the 40s: Jill and I watched a handful of crows crying out and attacking a red-tailed hawk high in the mare's-tails sky over Dayton Street.

2018: Charlotte, North Carolina to Savannah and Tybee Island, Georgia: Full sun and cold (frost on the windshield) throughout the area, patches of light snow and frozen swamp water between Columbia, South Carolina, all the way to Tybee Island, black ice on the streets of Savannah, snow remaining in the dunes, temperature near 40 degrees. In Yellow Springs, sleet and high near 30 degrees, snow tomorrow as a low-pressure system begins to dominate the week.

2019: Another soft day in the 50s, sunny, breezy. Jill and I smelled a faint odor of skunk as we walked toward Lawson Place. At Ellis Pond, 108 geese floating out on the water.

2020: Mild and cloudless day, a high of 47, robins clucking, crows cawing, one cardinal singing before dawn, geese gathered at the field across from Ellis, five mallards remaining on the pond so far through the winter. By the front porch, one Lenten rose plant has budded.

2021: Chris reports Trumpeter Swans near Columbus. At Ellis Pond, the great gathering of geese in two flocks, communing in the water, at least 300. Clouds continue to dominate the days of the new year.

> *Therefore all seasons shall be sweet to thee,*
> *Whether the summer clothe the general earth*
> *With greenness, or the redbreast sit and sing*
> *Betwixt the tufts of snow on the bare branch*
> *Of mossy apple tree, while the nigh thatch*
> *Smokes in the sun-thaw; whether the eve-drops fall*
> *Heard only in the trances of the blast;*
> *Or if the secret ministry of frost*
> *Shall hang them up in silent icicles,*
> *Quietly shining in the quiet moon.*

Samuel Taylor Coleridge

January 8th
The 8th Day of the Year

My diary seems to be a journal of the wind, sunshine and sky.

Charles Burchfield

Sunrise/set: 7:57/5:27
Day's Length: 9 hours 30 minutes
Average High/Low: 35/19
Average Temperature: 27
Record High: 64 – 2008
Record Low: - 11 – 1968

The Daily Weather
There is a 15 percent chance of mild weather today, as 85 percent of the highs for January 8th are in the 30s or below. Twenties occur 40 percent of the afternoons on this date, teens 15 percent, and single digits five percent. Lows reach below zero once every two decades. The sun shines half the time, offers rain or snow 40 percent of the time, a thunderstorm once in a quarter of a century.

Weather History for the Week Ahead
Weather history for the second week of January shows rapidly increasing odds for colder weather. Chances of highs only in the 20s or teens increase to near 50 percent on the 8th, 9th, 14th, and 15th. Below-zero readings occur most often on the 9th, 11th, and 16th (20 percent of the years in my record). With a general increase in the cold, skies have fewer clouds this week of the year, and the 12th, 13th, 15th and 16th bringing a 60 percent chance of sun. The cloudiest day of the week is usually the 14th, with only a 35 percent chance of clearing. Precipitation occurs two years out of three between the 12th and the 14th, with the 14th bringing snow to central Ohio more often than any other day of the entire year.

Natural Calendar
Under the white veneer of Deep Winter, the natural history year quickens. Nighttime excursions of skunks, the occasional appearance of flies, an increase in opossum activity, the prophetic calls of overwintering robins, the occasional passage of bluebirds, the great gatherings of Canadian geese for pairing, and the disappearance of autumn seeds all offer counterpoint to the subdued winter silence and the days of snow. And the arbitrary counterpoint of personal observations complements the seesaw moods of separate Januarys and the different characters of the various years

Daybook

1986: The first mother-of-millions bloomed at my office, late, perhaps, because of the tinted windows.

1987: Cardinals quiet throughout the day.

1993: Some geraniums, maybe a third of the plants, continue to bloom, while most seem dormant. I discovered a squirrel playing on the corn wheel today; he sat on the top of the post, reached up and took the corn cob in his paws, then, with his weight on the wheel, he toppled into a spin, hanging on, determined to get a few kernels before dropping to the snow.

1994: With Buttercup at the Covered Bridge: She romps in the snow, leaps over logs, bounds into the frozen swamp, delighting to break branches, bite the frozen leaves, feel her body overcome hills and rocks and fallen trees.

1996: To Mill Dam with Jeanie, Buttercup, and the new bulldog pup, Fergus: A foot of new snow on the ground (twenty-one days now of snow cover), the dogs charged through the drifts. The river was frozen solid above the dam. Sledders came across on the ice as we walked the ridge path. Halfway to the buzzard roost, a long line of geese flew over, heading north, maybe in search of open water. Then at the bend of the river, suddenly the whinny of robins: we had walked into a large flock overwintering. All around us, birds moved through the undergrowth feeding on the honeysuckle berries.

1998: After five days of weather in the 50s and 60s, the first opossum of the year was killed last night on Grinnell Road. Heavy rains and the warmth probably brought him out of hibernation. Worms were out too, forced from the ground by the water, the first time that I remember them so early in the year. The Little Miami is swollen to about three feet above normal, but it is still well within its banks. Heard a blue jay this morning with the crows; I love this warm January! Jeni called tonight: a thunderstorm in Bolivar, Ohio, a hundred miles north or Yellow Springs.

2001: Sweet gum seed balls have started to come down, maybe a fourth of them on the ground at school.

2002: To Columbus: Pure blue sky, shining snow in the fields, black crows, sharp northwest wind pushing on my back.

2004: Jeni reports being snowed in all week in Portland, Oregon, the airport shut down, schools and businesses closed.

2008: The last day of the thaw, highs in the lower 60s this morning. Walking with Jeff at the quarry, wind hard, my exhilaration from the flat glaciated bedrock, the quarry pools, flocks of geese feeding on the water, more flocks flying south overhead. After I got back, Jeff called to report sighting a buzzard over Cedarville. In the garden, two dead nettle plants have pink blossoms. The koi rose for food in the warm, record-breaking afternoon.

2009: A song sparrow on the north feeder this morning, the first one I've seen this winter in our yard. Two inches of snow on the ground, the sky pale blue gray, the village wintry. Squirrels chasing each other through the back trees.

2010: Eight inches of snow in the back yard, snow so light that it fell way from the shovel.

2012: Another bright and mild day. The moon rose out of the

northeast last night, set in the northwest this morning. Crows at 7:30 sharp. Chris photographed an open dandelion and put the picture on line.

2013: Red dawn, a cardinal singing at 8:04. High mackerel sky in midmorning, cardinals singing off and on through the day, a flock of maybe two score starlings hanging out by along Union Street. The young male cardinal that has attacked the windows of the camper since fall continues to bounce off the glass. Snow keeps on melting.

2016: Rain for today and tomorrow, then winter will finally arrive – at least for a week or so. News reports say that 2015 was the warmest year on record for the planet.

2017: I have neglected the bird feeders for a week or so, and the birds are slow to return. This morning, though, I had four doves in the yard, and I wonder if they have started to flock or if they flock at all.

2018: Tybee Island, Georgia to Merritt Island, Florida: The drive of about 300 miles finally brought us into the end of winter. A little below Jacksonville, the first signs, some clover and chickweed foliage and growth on several shrubs. The roadside grass seemed to become taller and greener as we went along, and when we reached Merritt Island, about halfway down the peninsula, we found that frost had not reached it (or had damaged very little), and there were a variety of plants in bloom, several violet azalea bushes in full flower; some bird-of-paradise; many bougainvilleas with blossoms; sidebeak pencilflower-like plant (or septicweed, *Senna occidentalis*) with large, yellow pea-like flowers; a few common wireweeds (*Sida acuta*); forget-me-nots; a yellow-flowered vetch; a red-headed three-seeded- mercury type of plant at the beach; several hibiscus flowers (with new growth beginning at the tips of some branches), poinsettias and two varieties of yellow-petaled rudbeckia-like plants (probably cucumberleaf sunflower (*Helianthus debilis*) and a variety of tickseed, a *Coreopsis*).

As to whether this place was the fulcrum of spring or the

other side of winter (the temperature falling to a borderland 34 in Titusville on the coldest days), I feel it was a place that would most likely remain safe from even more incursions of deep cold from the North and that when the warmth reawakened the land above Melbourne, the flowering of the new season would quickly spread to fill the Georgia and Carolina dun created by the unusual frost and snow of the past month. And the bitter weather of January's first week and the almost complete obliteration of flowers from South Carolina to the Gulf made it easier to find the relatively narrow space in which winter stalled (between Jacksonville and Melbourne) and in which the normal January flora of the peninsula could hold its own and then thrive as the days grow longer. Like the solstices, local borders of seasons often go unobserved, their effects only seen long after their occurrences. If the state of foliage is an astronomical gauge of the path of the sun, it is a complement and key to seasonal identity and perhaps to notions of personal identity, as well.

2019: Warm with a high of 61 today, soft morning, cardinals singing off and on, then the wind came up and blew steadily. At the pond, Jill counted 59 geese. Rick saw a small "orange and black butterfly" in the Glen today, maybe a *Polygonia*. Tonight a low of 24.

2020: Sun and below freezing. Cardinal calls at 7:35 this morning, crows follow almost immediately after. A note in the newspaper: 2019 was the second-warmest year and the past decade the warmest decade on record for the planet.
\

Journal

In January and February, I often fill my list books with fresh schedules. Sometimes, I put the whole year out before me, with projects for every month. Sometimes, though, I waver between dreams of the future and the myopia of hibernation.

On the one hand, I can count, if I choose, all the steps to spring. Everything lies out in promises so rich and sweet. Now dawn is coming earlier for the first time since June. In a few days, my gnomon will actually measure the turn of the Earth toward April; sunlight will fall just a little lower on my far north wall.

The year past, which ended with the collapse of the final autumn foliage, is already five weeks old. The dark morning sky already prophesies the summer: An hour before sunrise, Orion has set. Sirius has moved deep into the west, Cancer and Gemini following it. The Big Dipper is overhead. June's Arcturus is coming in from the east, and August's Vega has risen in the northeast

This week, the titmice will call. In two weeks, the owls will court, in three weeks the crows will become restless, in four weeks the cardinals will sing, in five weeks the doves will sing, in six weeks the skunk cabbage will be open, in seven weeks the sap will run in the maples, in eight weeks snowdrops will bloom, in nine weeks, the pussy willows will open, and then the aconites, and then the finches will turn gold. There is hardly time to get ready.

On the other hand, winter fever – like spring fever – short-circuits my ambitions. It convinces me to stretch out like the cats in front of the wood stove, to remain unthinking and still, to retreat into the moment, to be here alone and rest and sleep. There is challenge enough to come, the fever tells me: conflict, passion, pain, encounter. The road ahead is fast and cluttered and loud; the end is certain and hard. I should stay here and be cleansed and cherished. Winter is an angel, my body says; winter lasts forever; hide beneath its wings.

January 9th
The 9th Day of the Year

I used to harbor the thought that one year of Nature chronology would finish the job - would rob succeeding years of new chronologies. Even though I walk forever on the same paths and in the same woods and fields, and even note the same phenomena, each year will bring a new chronology, for my view of life is ever changing.

Charles Burchfield, *Journal*, January 9, 1915

Sunrise/set: 7:57/5:28
Day's Length: 9 hours 31 minutes
Average High/Low: 35/19
Average Temperature: 27
Record High: 61 – 1939
Record Low: - 6 – 1982

The Daily Weather

The high temperature falls into the 20s more often (50 percent of the time) today than on any other day in the entire year. The other 50 percent is divided between 40s (30 percent of the time), 30s (15 percent) and single digit highs (five percent). There is a 15 percent chance of a morning below zero, one of the highest chances of the winter. And today begins the peak below-zero period for Ohio, which lasts until the 21st. January 9 is one of the two clearest days of the month -- the 26th is the other; both carry a 60 percent chance of sunshine. The likelihood for precipitation is relatively low, only 25 percent.

Natural Calendar

No matter the cold, beavers strip bark for food along the rivers. Skunks come out to root in the ground during mid-winter thaws. The tufted titmouse begins its spiral mating flights. Blue jays give their bell-like calls. Sometimes a fly emerges indoors from a potted plant.

Daybook

1987: The number of birds at the feeders seems lower this year.

My mother says the same thing in Madison, and Uncle Bill in Minnesota.

1989: Sparrows in abundance at the feeders, but no juncos or song sparrows.

1993: Crows loud in the back trees for about five minutes at dawn. Four blue jays at the bird feeder today, more than I've ever seen together. One female, three males, I think. Finches getting more aggressive, the least fearful of the winter feeders.

1994: Temperatures have stayed below freezing most of the days since Christmas Eve, all the garden frozen, the flowering cabbage keeping its shape, still standing tall, red and blue. Birds less common at the feeder. Finches sporadic. Sparrows less common than some years. The families of chickadees and cardinals remain faithful. At the Covered Bridge, the river is frozen over in places, the open water deep blue under the clear sky.

1998: Jeni reports a second thunderstorm in Bolivar, a hundred miles north of Yellow Springs. She said the sides of her apartment building were shaking from the force of the sound waves. Along the coast in the Northeast: ice storms and power outages; in the Southeast: heavy rains and floods.

2000: One daffodil, an inch high, pushing through the ground by the front sidewalk.

2004: Geese flew over the house in the dark this morning, 7:35. At South Glen, I saw the effects of last week's flood in the leaves woven into the fences, piles of debris caught in fallen branches all along the paths. The river had come up over ten feet in some places, and the water flowed deep into the flood plain, hundreds and hundreds of yards in some places. Above me, two hawks screamed and swooped. A pileated woodpecker called from the trees, a Carolina wren from the bushes. Crows flew by.

2005: Last week's high water is down. Mike walked all the way to Jacoby a few days ago, said there had been no danger to his dogs.

Cardinal song off and on throughout today. Snow shut down Seattle and northern California.

2007: The first snowfall of the year overnight, about an inch on the grass. Most of it melted in the afternoon sun.

2008: A little movement toward spring: I heard a cardinal sing about 10:00 this morning; Don's daylilies were starting to come up, and a few peonies in the back yard showed their red tips. A downy woodpecker came to the suet this afternoon, the first downy I've seen all winter.

2009: A cardinal sang once at 7:33 this morning. A titmouse heard southeast of the alley a little after 9:00. Ed Oxley called, said he had snowdrops up about an inch. Another song sparrow feeding today. Squirrels running around in the woods.

2011: Crows at 7:44 this morning.

2012: Yet another sunny and mild day, with Madison, Wisconsin even warmer! Walking downtown, I saw five buzzards circling the village. A cardinal was singing near the post office, and Jeanie heard a blue jay in the back yard while I was gone. It just called again at 10:45 a.m.

2014: Crows at 7:36 this morning. In the alley, the bittersweet berries have darkened and shriveled in the below-zero weather this past weekend. Near Lawson Place, the cold seems to have brought down hundreds of sweet gum seed balls, the snowy ground littered with their prickly shells.

2016: In the wake of a very warm start to the year, Ed Oxley left me a message about how he had been walking along the path in the park near his property this morning, and "I saw a little hump on the blacktop, looked down and saw that the lump was a little toad. I picked it up and carried it to the woodpile, put it under some leaves. It must have come out with all the rain and warm weather we've been having. Pretty unusual!" And John Blakelock called to tell me one of his hellebores was blooming. In my dooryard, white tips of the snowdrops are quite prominent, and my own hellebores, white and violet, are in full March flowering.

2018: Having found or pretended to find the lacuna between winter and spring, I walk the beach at Merritt Island, Florida, the rhythm and the scent of the waves here are somehow like the daybook journal of home itself, pulling me back and forth from one year to another in a sequence of memories anchored in the single image and blend of emotions that follow the warm eastern Atlantic, place knitting time into fabric: sand and love and water and defeat and success and loss and renewal and ennui and spring-out-of-season and acceptance and soft happiness.

2022: Chris writes from his farm nearby: "This morning, I took a walk through our woods and the trails on our prairie ground. Down at the lowest elevation of our property there is a spur of woods that conceals a small vernal pool. As I was walking down there, I looked in. The boggy area was so rich with bright green grass; it just invited me in.

"And right there, I suddenly had the notion to slip in there and pray Terce. So I did. The bog was frozen solid—just a little rust-red trickle of spring water through the midst of jade green grass and frozen black muck. The woods encircled it on all sides, like pillars of a temple. It was strange and wonderful, as if I was seeing the spot for the first time.

"I got to Ps. 121—'and now our feet are standing/within your gates, O Jerusalem"—and suddenly it struck me: the notion of Jerusalem right there, beneath my feet, surrounding me. I finished the rest of the psalm in tears, praying for the creaturely world: "For the peace of Jerusalem pray/peace be to your homes. May peace reign in your walls/in your palaces, peace. For love of my brethren and friends/I say, peace upon you. For love of the house of the Lord/I will ask for your good."'

These are the days
The sun
Is swimming back
to the east
and the light on the water
gleams
as never, it seems, before.

Mary Olive

January 10th
The 10th Day of the Year

Each of us carries an inward map on which are inscribed, as on Renaissance charts, the seas and continents known to us. On my own map, the regions where I have lived most attentively are crowded with detail....

Scott Russell Sanders

Sunrise/set: 7:57/5:29
Day's Length: 9 hours 32 minutes
Average High/Low: 34/19
Average Temperature: 27
Record High: 59 – 1890
Record Low: - 15 – 1982

The Daily Weather

Today's odds: Five percent chance of highs in the 50s, twenty percent chance of highs in the 40s, thirty-five percent of 30s, twenty-five percent of 20s, ten to 15 percent of teens or single digits, and a slight chance for a high below zero. The sun appears half of the days in my record, and the likelihood of precipitation is 50 percent, twice as great as it was yesterday. Below-zero lows occur three years in twenty.

Natural Calendar

On January 10th, even though dawn remains at its latest time of the year, the cardinals have become a little bolder, sometimes calling a full half hour before daylight. By the middle of February, sunrise has moved about half an hour from its early January schedule, and cardinals sing by 7:00 o'clock (Eastern Standard Time) in Yellow Springs. By the end of the first week of March, they call at 6:30 a.m. By the end of March, they are up at 6:00. By the third week in April, they sing even earlier, their mating song beginning at 5:00.

Toward the end of May, summer has arrived, and most cardinals reach their limit around 4:00 a.m. Mating territories have been set and defended. Now the longest days of the year begin, fulfillment of the spring vigil.

Daybook

1982: Record temperature: 15 below zero, and wind chill of 55 below, worst cold wave since the late 1800s, coldest day of the 20th century in the Midwest. Jeni went out (for her birthday) in the storm, got home safely in spite of some problems with the car.

1993: Gray morning, the crackle of sleet on the greenhouse windows. I'm wearing my father's brown wool jacket; my mother's Irish shawl over my legs. The fire hot across the room, burning the scrap I cut yesterday. The salt truck passes by, yellow lights spinning. Sparrows at the feeder in spite of the storm, crows fly over, pause in a tree on Limestone Street. I check the weather graph: sleet or snow today over the past four years, and not a glimpse of sun.

1998: After a week of warm weather, the garlic I planted in late November has sprouted - and a few sprouts are even up three inches. In the back trees, the crows are loud this afternoon, louder than I think I've heard them so far this winter. Ragged cumulus clouds pass quickly over as the January 10th cold front comes through, even some sun for the first time in days.

2000: Thunderstorm and hail, hard winds before sunrise. Gusts to fifty miles an hour around 11:00 a.m.

2004: Crows seen this morning, the sightings becoming more frequent.

2007: The news reports that 2006 was the warmest year on record for the United States. At school in Wilmington, I saw angleworms stranded on the parking lot from the rain.

2008: Hard rains for the last 24 hours, the Little Miami high.

2009: Ed Oxley said he had a huge flock of starlings around his house this morning. Snow storms across the northern tier of states. Extreme cold in Alaska forecast to move here in a few days.

2010: Bitter cold and snow for several days now. This morning, bittersweet hulls and berries covered the sidewalk near Limestone Street. Hoar frost holds fast to all the trees and shrubs. One robin heard when I walked out the front door.

2012: Another beautiful day of sun and highs near 50 degrees. More daffodil spears pushing up in the dooryard garden. Matt Mindy wrote: "I'm sure you yourself and others have noticed, but I saw forsythia blossoms opening up at the corner of Whiteman and Xenia. Really spring-like weather. I don't know what this will mean for spring when it actually arrives."

2013: As I was getting out of the shower this morning at 7:30, I heard a cardinal sing loud and long. Out in the yard, snowdrops are up about and inch, and the handful of daffodil buds that had formed in late November appeared unhurt by the late December and early January cold. In the alleys, blue jays have been calling throughout my walks.

2014: Soft, wet snow overnight, melting now. At 7:35: Crows and cardinals calling in the distance.

2016: After a warm start to the year: Rain before dawn, then hard wind and fat snowflakes. At 10:20 a.m., tree branches were covered with snow, the air crisp, the air still. At 11:15 Dennie Eagleton called to say she had just seen a pod of about forty sandhill cranes flying over Glen Helen toward the southwest.

2017: Strong south wind today, temperature above freezing for the first time in days. Highs in the 50s forecast for the next two days. Rain. Crows on the move above the road to Springfield as I was both coming and going.

2018: Melbourne and Titusville, Florida: Spanish needles (*Bidens pilosa*) or romerillo (*Bidens alba*), the most common wildflower of the area this time of year, and large-leafed sorrel in the apartment enclosure. At the nature preserve north of Titusville, several bulltongue arrowhead in bloom, *Sagittaria lancifolia;* a sprawling, large-flowered aster mostly gone to seed – probably a climbing aster, *Ampelaster carolinianus)* –perhaps the very last flower of the old year; a couple of scarlet milkweeds (*Asclepias curassavica)* in late flower; a shrub with unopened white flowers (at midafternoon) with the look of a love or lace vine.

2019: Emily Foubert writes: "Have you ever been walking and all of the sudden you are surrounded by birds on all sides, and you can't help but pause and ask what they are up to? Well, that happened to me on this day. The house finch were feeding on the ground, then chickadees swooped in and called curiously at eye level. A female cardinal, I then noticed, was not but five steps from me in the leaves, perfectly camouflaged except for her red beak. Then a sole brown creeper popped on in to the thicket, wagging its way through the trunks.

"That day though, it was the sounds that really caught my attention. The chickadees and titmice were singing their spring songs!! And the most surprising songster of all? The white breasted nuthatch. A new, happy and playful 'younking' laugh twirled out of few different beaks. 'Their spring song,' I mused. And they are usually very shy. But on that warm day they were dancing all around the branches, calling and singing their new song. I mostly stay away from anthropomorphizing bird's feelings, but today I could FEEEEEEL their blissful joy within me."

And Leanne reports that she saw hundreds of vultures at roadkills along the highway between Clifton and Yellow Springs: another rite of winter and spring.

2020: Sue Brezine writes: "Robins gather more than once a day at my birdbath. They number 4, 5, 7, and the most 9. Clucking at each other, sometimes patiently wait their turn to bathe in the warmed water. Pure delight." Leslie reports buzzards roosting in her trees, their flocking still obvious, juncos still coming to her feeder.

As human beings, we like meaning in our lives. We like it so much we will come up with all kinds of ways to make sure it is found. The movements of the stars mirror our actions here on earth, magic numbers will influence our destinies, and the nature of our blood is the lifeblood of our natures. In each case, all we need is a set of principles to unlock the code. This almanac itself is a very good example.

Liza Dalby, writing about a 17th century Chinese almanac

January 11th
The 11th Day of the Year

I love to wade and flounder through the swamp now, these bitter cold days when the snow lies deep on the ground. I penetrate to islets inaccessible in summer, where the alder berry glows yet and the azalea buds, and perchance a single tree sparrow or a chickadee lisps by my side. There is but little life and but few objects, it is true. We are reduced to admire buds, even like the partridges.... Even a little shining bud which lies sleeping behind its twig and dreaming of spring, perhaps half concealed by ice, is object enough.

Henry David Thoreau, January 10, 1856

Sunrise/set: 7:56/5:30
Day's Length: 9 hours 34 minutes
Average High/Low: 34/19
Average Temperature: 27
Record High: 67 – 1890 an 2020
Record Low: - 14 – 1886

The Daily Weather
Below-zero temperatures occur 25 percent of all the mornings on this date; that's the highest percentage for any day in an Ohio winter. Highs, however reach into the 50s or 60s ten percent of the time. Forties occur a fourth of the days in my record, 30s twenty-five percent of the time, 20s ten percent, teens 25 percent, single digits five percent. The sun shines half the days, and rain or snow falls four years in a decade.

Natural Calendar
On the hillsides, the springs are clear and the vegetation bright when the snow has melted. New chickweed covers parts of the bottomland. Basal foliage of sweet rocket and leafcup is lush and tall, waiting for April and May. Wood mint is growing back.

On January 11, Yellow Springs sunrise time – which remains at its latest time of the year between December 31 and January 10 (7:57 a.m.) – finally starts to occur earlier. It will continue to recede until June 8, when it reaches 5:06 a.m. Sunrise remains at that time until June 22, when the slide toward winter begins once again.

A few hours before sunrise, the sky appears the way it will be on the warm evenings of middle May. Arcturus is the brightest star overhead, followed by the Corona Borealis. To the east are August's Vega and Cygnus. The only remnants of winter are Castor and Pollux setting in the northwest.

Daybook

1985: First fox sparrow seen at the bird feeder, large and beautiful.

1988: Geese fly over at 5:00 p.m.

1989: Cardinal sings at 7:30 a.m., the sky still dark: the earliest I've heard it on a Deep Winter morning, a hint of Late Winter coming.

1990: I sometimes feel if I can make the record long enough, and if I can include enough, the fragments of my life will come together. If I can lay the pieces out in a row, day after day, I'll be able to understand their sequence and their part in the whole, and my part.

1991: Sparrows swarm near the east forsythia, chatter and quarrel half an hour before sunset.

1993: I worked in the yard this afternoon splitting wood, the sparrows quiet and aloof, no cardinals, the ground sodden, absorbing the sound of my axe, trees hung with ice.

1994: After temperatures almost to zero, the yellow witch hazel petals on Dayton street still hang on, but they have withered and darkened.

2002: Gray, gentle, misty morning: the grass and fields seem like the soft, tan coat of a vast beast.

2004: Crows flew silently over the house again this morning around 8:00. Then a cardinal called out, and I heard a wren chatter.

2005: The warm, wet January continues. There was even thunder this afternoon. Eight inches of rain so far this year.

2007: Doves in full song at about 9:00 a.m. when I walked Bella through the alley.

2008: The mornings have been quiet when I walked Bella. The starlings that used to sit in Don's tree during December have been gone most of this new year.

2009: A large flock of starlings settled over Greg's locust and black walnut trees at 10:00 this morning.

2011: Crows at 7:40 this morning, snow beginning at about 8:00. The news says that 49 out of the 50 United States have snow cover recorded this week. Other reports: Last year was the wettest on record in the world, and a tie with 2005 for the warmest.

2012: Heavy rain this morning, washing away the rest of the snow. A high in the lower 60s here, record cold in Los Angeles, record heat in Florida.

2017: After yesterday's mild temperatures, heavy rain and wind, I saw a skunk had been killed overnight on the highway south. Record snowfall over a foot at Jeni's house in Portland.

2018: Melbourne, Florida: Warm and sunny in the 80s, the second-last day before the arrival of a cold front. Cloudy and 56 in Yellow Springs, also the second-last day before the arrival of a cold front. At a nature preserve near Cocoa Beach: many dead fish in the water; several large flocks of white herons; an apparently simple habitat of hardy shrubs with red berries and grass similar to Johnson grass. Several butterflies seen, one mosquito. Black medic was the only wildflower, along with a few Spanish needles. And at 4:02 this afternoon, Mike wrote from Yellow Springs: "I just wanted to report that I saw and heard two of sandhill cranes that flew over the corner of Whiteman and Phillips Streets at about one o'clock this afternoon. I was surprised I could see them, as cloudy as it was…."

2019: Winter Storm Gaia approaches, due tonight. The pond has started to freeze over, and the flock of Canadian geese has retreated to the field across the road. The swamp chestnut oak, the shingle oak and the red oak in the oak grove still hold most of their leaves, all curled and crisp. Along the stream near the soybean field, hemlock is only an inch long.

2020: Mild and rainy, tying a record high of 67 degrees today. The hydrangea bushes I planted after Thanksgiving have sent up foliage, lungwort has new spring leaves, and a few mock orange buds are greening. Robins heard peeping in the morning, a common occurrence now.

2021: A storm all across the Southeast at lunar perigee, but only a steady barometer here, the gray winter held in place by high pressure.

2023: California continues to be battered by heavy winds and rain storms, flooding widespread from San Francisco south. The European Union Climate Change Service reports that the last eight years were the warmest on record, with 2016 the hottest. Jill sent a photo of a tulip pushing up an inch in her yard, and I found the first daffodils emerging around my garden. John Blakelock sends a haiku: "In January/ 6 A.M in a dark time/No birds are singing,"

Journal

Every winter, the two koi in our small pond stop feeding when the water temperature reaches the low 40s. Both fish are about a foot long. Zelda is a golden orange, Emmett is white with black markings. They lie side by side in the deepest water near the pump, slowly moving their fins but not responding when I walk close to them.

Zelda and Emmett seem to have no worries. This is their eighth winter in the pond. They seem to know that there is nothing they can do to change the course of the season. There is nothing they can do if the pump stops working or if the pond freezes solid in a long cold wave or if I simply forget about them. Day after day, they remain motionless facing west waiting for spring as though they really do know that April will bring the mild west winds that will eventually quicken them.

Sometimes, I wonder if they have reached enlightenment and if they have transcended passion and desire. Do they instinctively count their breaths or the cold fronts or the sunsets? Do they remember spring and the warmth of the water?

I find myself jealous of their winter season, of their apparent indifference to danger, of their ability to use the cold to their advantage. I am jealous of their single-mindedness, of their resignation, of their deep patience, endurance and trust. I am jealous of their bodies that simply tell them to look west, to expect the warming future.

And it came to me all in a feeling how everything fitted together, the place and ourselves and the animals and the tools, and how the sky held us. I saw how sweetly we were enabled by the land and the animals and our few simple tools.

Wendell Berry

January 12th
The 12th Day of the Year

The cherished fields
Put on their winter-robe of purest white.
'Tis brightness all; save where the new snow melts
Along the mazy current. Low the woods
Bow their hoary head; and, ere the languid sun
Faint from the west emits his evening ray,
Earth's universal face, deep-hid and chill,
Is one wild dazzling waste, that buries wide
The works of man.

James Thomson

Sunrise/set: 7:56/5:31
Day's Length: 9 hours 35 minutes
Average High/Low: 34/19
Average Temperature: 27
Record High: 68 – 1890 (63 – 2017)
Record Low: - 16 – 1918

The Daily Weather

Today's temperature distribution: five percent chance of 60s, five percent of 50s, twenty percent of 40s, thirty-five percent of 30s, fifteen percent of 20s, fifteen percent of teens, five percent for single digits. Below zero mornings occur once or twice in a decade. Chances of rain are 30 percent, 15 percent for snow. The sun appears 60 percent of the days in my record.

Natural Calendar

Yellow perch are usually caught through the month of January in shallow Grand Lake St. Mary's, almost a hundred miles northwest of Yellow Springs. In the muddy Ohio River, sauger are biting. Throughout the region, the last euonymus berries continue to fall, marking the passage of winter as they disappear. The habits of starlings change slightly, still in flocks, but moving more to town as if in a prequel to pairing for mating.

1986: Sycamore Hole was perfectly quiet this afternoon, no wind, no bird song, no movement to the water, but cold, deep blue reflection of the sky, bright sun on the white trees.

1993: This morning by the fire an hour and a half before sunrise: The back trees outlined against the fog through the neighbors' porch lights. Freezing rain in the street. The sky is pale as if there were a moon behind it. Dawns wet and gray all month; the yard is cocooned in dull vapor and damp cold.

2004: The winter has been mild, but the flowering kale is finally well past its best. The Japanese honeysuckle holds its color, but the leaves curl in the morning frost. In the garden, some foliage still holds on the butterfly bush and the small-flowered hollyhocks. The rains of a week ago have bared the red tips of a few peonies. Out in the country, the fields are soft brown. I love driving south to Washington Court House in the early morning, the sun orange and low - in my eyes, but welcome. The farm ponds are frozen now. Few birds cross in front of me as I travel, only sometimes a small flock of geese or crows. I haven't noticed the large gatherings of starlings this week. Has their flocking ended? Are they starting to pair off for mating? Any minute the movement to spring will become visible, fragments emerging from the fog of these days.

2005: The sky cleared a little for the first time all year, and the temperature rose to 64. I walked at Jacoby with Bella. The river was flooding for the second time in a week (it had receded by the 7th, then rose again after yesterday's rain). At the landing, the water was fast and muddy, but up the side of the hill, the springs were clear and the vegetation bright. New chickweed covered parts of the bottomland. Sweet rocket and leafcup were lush and tall. Wood mint was coming back. Some skunk cabbage was open. As I walked along the swamp, a small, pale moth followed me, and I found a large, four-inch crayfish crawling along through the shallow water.

2007: Walking with Bella at South Glen: The air was soft, the sky overcast, temperature a little over 50. Crows and starlings were calling. Clusters of euonymus berries had fallen recently to the ground, an acceleration in the progress of their cycle. A few buds of one multiflora rose bush were pushing out, their tips flushed pink.

2008: A mild, partly sunny day in the 40s. I worked around the yard, found the first snowdrops and daffodils up almost an inch. Almost all the euonymus berries have fallen. Small white aster plants have lost all their seeds.

2009: Cardinal song from 7:35 until about 7:45 this morning, then crows until about 8:00. Cloudy with temperature in the 20s, two inches of snow from overnight.

2011: Rick writes: "Hey Bill, I finally saw who the mystery feather-maker is in the garage. And you were right, an owl. A tiny screech owl making that great big mess. He/she gets a bird almost every night. Grabs a small bird off its roost and swoops up into the rafters away from the elements and bigger owls. However, I wasn't quite so thrilled went I went out this morning, to find red feathers all over my little white car. He/she can have all the sparrows they want, but …."

2013: Another very soft morning, crows at 7:55, blue jays whining, starlings chirping and chattering, one robin peeping, one cardinal calling.

2014: At the college, several daffodils have shoots two or three inches high next to the King Center.

2015: Portland, Oregon, temperature steady in the 40s and 50s for at least the past week: In Yellow Springs, deep cold below zero, beginning to warm a little. Here in Oregon, south past Salem, I walked at a small city park: moss growing, lichens growing, catkins emerged on a variety of birch, deep green holly, a few stunted sow thistles budded. At the church, daffodils were up about an inch. Along Jeni's fence umbels of pink buds at the end of red-brown stems with thick, deep evergreen, opposite, not clasping, entire (but wavy) leaves.

2016: In the midst of snow bursts, starlings (the first time I've seen them in the yard since autumn) joined the cardinals, sparrows, doves, cowbirds, and a red-bellied woodpecker feeding today.

2017: Rain through the night, south winds: The temperature was 63 when I woke up, the house cooler than the outside air. Walking to Jill's, we found a worm that had been driven from the earth and stranded on the sidewalk by the rain. I noticed that the red burning bush berries were all over the sidewalk, the bush at least half empty – like the bittersweet, and the hard, spiked fruits of the sweet gum tree at the end of Davis Street had started to come down. At around 2:00 this afternoon, heavy rain and wind, thunder and lightning, the first thunderstorm of the year.

2018: Almost an inch of snow in Yellow Springs today, but on Merritt Island, the temperature was in the 80s with a cool ocean breeze.

2019: Winter Storm Gaia has brought all-day snow, the first real heavy snow (eight inches) of this winter. By the post office, the small fruits of the decorative pear trees continue to scatter to the road and sidewalk in the wind.

2020: After a high of 67 and rain throughout the day, a cold front came through in the night with hard winds. Now it is chilly but quiet. Cardinal song at 7:35, crows at 7:45 this morning. So far, January is 13 degrees above normal.

2021: Few birds at the feeder for several days. Hawks or cats? The Anthropocene? More articles appearing in the newsfeed about the galloping extinction of insects. I lit seven candles on my 12-candle winter wreath this morning, double-counting to make sure I was getting the number right, realizing how soon Early Spring would be here. Returning to my desk, I see that the sparrows are haunting the bushes outside my window, not extinct after all.

2022: George Bieri called to tell me he had seen half a dozen sandhill cranes flying south, coming low at the level of the canopy.

He said his daughter, Louisa, saw about fifty of them flying high over the Vale about a week ago.

2023: A thunderstorm this morning before sunrise, strong booms in the sky nearby, then heavy rain. The cold front moved in. by the middle of the afternoon.

Journal

Over the years, I have paid attention to starlings, both as visitors to my yard and also as creators of dramatic murmurations that dive and spin through the winter. Their behavior in and around Yellow Springs does not always keep a strict schedule, and many of their activities overlap from season to season, but my scattered records reflect something of their periodic movements.

After spending the late autumn and early winter in great flocks that visit and feast in the fields throughout the township (and much of the nation), starlings frequently break into smaller groups early in the year.

Sometimes, as they did on January 4, 2012, the first small flock comes down from the woods to eat suet in my yard. On January 12 of 2016, in the midst of snowbursts, the first starlings joined the cardinals, sparrows, doves, cowbirds, chickadees, tufted titmice and a red-bellied woodpecker at my birdfeeder.

I have notes from the middle of February about clusters of starlings visiting the neighborhood more frequently, even courting then, and it seems that most of the larger flocks have broken up and pairing has begun by March 1.

On March 4, 1991, I noticed "doves making a nest in a back locust tree. Starlings were nesting in holes in the limbs of the same tree." And from that point forward through the years, I have sometimes seen starlings attacking the shiny flashing of my chimney, trying to be sure that not even phantom birds could encroach upon their space.

Starlings complete courtship in March and April, at least along High Street, and by May 15, the first fledglings have emerged to whine and beg for food – which they do, depending on the permissiveness of the parents, throughout June and into July.

Then, by the middle of August, I notice the high wires filling with the *Sturnus vulgaris* and the first murmurations dancing in the sky. Some starling families do remain in the village, clucking, chirping, burbling, and whistling through the autumn and early winter. Usually, however, by the beginning of November, there are fewer small flocks in Yellow Springs trees, and most of the birds gather to soar and feed as one until the sun starts to rise earlier in the morning and the breeding cycle divides and scatters their winter assemblies.

January 13th
The 13th Day of the Year

There is in all visible things an invisible fecundity, a dimmed light, a meek namelessness, a hidden wholeness…. There is in all things an inexhaustible sweetness and purity, a silence that is a fount of action and joy. It rises up in wordless gentleness and flows out to me from the unseen roots of all created being, welcoming me tenderly, saluting me with indescribable humility.

Thomas Merton

Sunrise/set: 7:56/5:32
Day's Length: 9 hours 36 minutes
Average High/Low: 34/19
Average Temperature: 26
Record High: 67 – 1890
Record Low: - 9 – 1912

The Daily Weather
Although the sun appears for at least a few hours on more than half the January 13ths, rain or snow comes 60 percent of the time, making today one of the wetter days in my January weather history. Temperatures are in the 60s five percent of the time, in the 50s five percent, the 40s thirty percent, the 30s forty percent, the 20s fifteen percent, the single digits five percent. Mornings below zero are rare on this date.

Natural Calendar
Opossums and raccoons become more active in milder Januarys, and they appear at night along country roads. Skunk cabbage is up in the swamps, blackened by the cold but still strong. Watercress holds in the streams. Where the ground is not frozen, new mint grows under the protection of a southern hedge or wall. In the pastures, basal leaves of thistles and mullein are deep green beneath the snow. In town, winter-blooming hellebores and Chinese witch hazels blossom in the warmest microclimates.

1984: Walk at John Bryant with Neysa on her sled. Ground frozen, covered with maybe three inches of snow. Craneflies swarming despite the freezing temperatures. The pond solid and white, plain without its ducks and geese.

1987: Cardinal heard 7:35 a.m. and 8:15 a.m.

1988: Waxing moon in Taurus, one day before full moon: seven big chubs caught, including a new record, ten-inch, half-pound chub. Bobwhite heard. Kingfishers race up river. Tufted titmouse seen.

1990: Cardinals sing off and on all day.

1991: Hawthorn berries falling steadily.

1993: Only a few hours of sun so far in 1993. This morning, before the total gray took hold, a band of golden clouds in the east, bright for a few minutes, then the sky was covered with fog and rain. No cardinals these mornings, silence except for the occasional squabbling of sparrows, crows passing though once in a while.

1994: At the Covered Bridge, the faster water of the Little Miami was still open, black and brown under the dark sky. I walked the ridge, breaking honeysuckle branches, making a path for spring and finding vantage points from which to watch for bluebells and twinleaf.

1996: I took our two bulldogs out for a walk at the old mill yesterday morning. It had snowed a few more inches over night for a total of several feet in some places, and we were the first to get all the way to the dam.

The older bulldog was invigorated by the cold, ranged on ahead, leaping fallen trees, racing back from time to time for reassurance. The puppy, six months old, had to break trail with his chest.

Above the dam, the river was frozen over. Below, in the open channel that led to the mill, the water was black and the current strong and loud. Half way to the old sycamore where vultures roost in spring and fall, a formation of geese flew over heading north. Then at the bend of the river, suddenly there was a whinny of robins, and we walked right into the middle of the large flock that has been here feeding on honeysuckle berries since October. The birds moved through the undergrowth on both sides of the path, calling and playing.

2004: In the greenhouse, the jade tree flowers have come to the end of their cycle, the white petals rusting. Outside in the east garden, snowdrops have come up, some with their pale white bud-like tips showing.

2007: An inch of rain overnight and this morning, flooding the yard. In the alley, some purple deadnettle has budded. In the east garden, snowdrops seem ready to flower, their white buds prominent. All around the property, daffodil, hyacinth, and crocus foliage is emerging.

2008: Crows at 8:05 a.m. A downy woodpecker came to the suet again. A cluster of sparrow feathers found by the large bird feeder; yesterday, I found another scattering of feathers by the coral bell garden: the red-tailed hawk that I saw yesterday afternoon most likely was the culprit. Squirrels seen chasing each other on a box elder tree near the alley this morning.

2009: Low barometric pressure this morning, snow melting from the branches, ice and water falling to the snow on the ground, pock marking. Deep cold on the way, only a thin break of blue in the clouds at 9:00 this morning, then the gray closed over for the day. Derek cut up the white mulberry branch that fell when Hurricane Ike came through in September. More wood for the winter. In the greenhouse, the amaryllis is at its peak, deep red. The jade tree hasn't bloomed for years. The three coleus I brought in at the end of September are holding on, growing just little.

2010: Tufted titmouse singing this morning about 7:30, a cardinal heard about 9:30, the first one in months. Sun and clear blue skies all day long.

2011: Crows at 7:50 this morning. Peter says the two overwintering sandhill cranes are still here.

2012: A small flock of starlings has settled in to feed with the other birds today, the second small flock to land in the yard since fall.

2013: As a strong cold front approaches, the day is warm in the low 60s with light rain. In the north garden, two daffodils are breaking open, the first time I've ever seen them start to bloom so early.

2014: Crows at 7:53 this morning. Mild, 50 degrees, southwest wind. Walked south of Cedarville with Jeff, robins peeping off and on the whole way.

2017: Rochester, NY: No snow between here and Yellow Springs, and, in fact, the roadside grasses became greener as we drove across northern Ohio and New York. When we reached the city, a long flock of crows flew over, augmenting the sense of the weakening winter.

2018: At Cocoa Beach this morning, I photographed a yellow hawkweed-like flower, with a two-foot reddish stem and fat, short, clasping, opposite leaves. Drove from Cocoa Beach to Palatka in north Florida, through the Ocala National Forest, where frost had burned many of the ferns and deciduous bushes. At the St. John's River: sun and cold in the 50s. In the yard of the motel, I found the round, white seed heads of a handful of dandelions. Teens and single digits again in Yellow Springs.

2019: Snow finally stopping, nine inches total. First dove seen in the yard this winter.

2020: Mild 40s, cardinal at 7:37 a.m. A note from Jane: "Today there were two snowdrops in bloom and numerous heads! Spring marches toward us."

2021: Emily Foubert writes: "Well, Spring seems to be here today!

January 13 and every bird seems to be singing their spring song at my sit spot this morning. From 10-11:30am I heard both types of cardinal songs (cheer what what what, and birdie birdie birdie), Goldfinch song, titmice song, drumming of woodpeckers (their "song"), White throated sparrow song, and the chickadee's "spring's here!" song. And the best part came When I saw two red shouldered hawk's mating in a tree and proclaiming it with many "keer"'s and screeches. I also want to note to you that I heard the cardinal's "cheer what what what" song in Jan 6th! Is that early?"

2023: More daffodils seen: Don's are two or three inches high. Wild onions growing. And sandhill cranes continue to fly over: Valerie and her son saw about 45 sandhills as they flew over the Glass Farm area at 12:50 p.m. today. Just before 1:00 p.m. on the 13th, Kitty must have hear heard the same sedge (flock).
"I just heard sandhill cranes to the west," she wrote.. "Did not see them, but the sounds continued for a minute or so, seeming like a large group."

The ricks and trees stand silent in the moon,
Loaded with snow, and tiny drift from branches
Slip to the ground in woods with sliding sigh.
Private the woods, enjoying a secret beauty.

Vita Sackville-West, *The Land*

January 14th
The 14th Day of the Year

The place to observe nature is where you are; the walk you take today is the walk you took yesterday.

John Burroughs

Sunrise/set: 7:55/5:34
Day's Length: 9 hours 39 minutes
Average High/Low: 34/19
Average Temperature: 26
Record High: 68 – 1932
Record Low: - 2 – 1994

The Daily Weather

Snow falls on half the January 14ths in my record, making today one of the three snowiest days in January (the 22nd and 24th being the other two). Highs in the 60s come once every two decades, 40s thirty percent of the time, 30s twenty percent, 20s thirty-five percent, teens ten percent. Completely overcast conditions occur almost half of the years.

Natural Calendar

Potatoes are often cut today and dusted with sulfur to prevent rot. They are then dried and allowed to sprout in flats. Perennials should be covered with extra mulch if they are sprouting early. Vines, shade and fruit trees may be pruned after a week or two of averages below freezing.

Daybook

1987: Cardinal sang at 8:45 a.m. No chubs caught today in the river, nothing but small shiners; they are all that ever take my bait from now until February. Kingfishers flew back and forth while I watched my bobber.

1993: Monotony of the gray Yellow Springs winter, sunless days, flurries, light rain. The rivers are high and fast. It's been too cold for the wheat and roadside grass to be turning green like they did last year. No storms. The heavy snow passes north, the deep freezes stay above Chicago. Even the sleet is mild, the ice easily weakened by salt. The birds are quiet, as if they were subdued by this solemn procession of clouds and weak barometric fronts.

1996: To the Mill Dam: Snow melting, temperatures in the 40s, sun shining. Robins still here, crows restless, sparrows, starlings, cardinals, chickadees active in the clear, warm afternoon. For the past few mornings at home, it seems the birds have been more visible and audible. They read the gnomon of the sun in the trees like I read it on the wall by my desk.

2001: Camelback cricket found halfway up the bedroom wall.

2004: Camelback cricket killed by the dog on the kitchen floor this morning. Outside by the south fence, the color of all the Osage fruits has changed from chartreuse to muddy brown.

2005: Cardinal song remains strong near 7:30 these mornings, then off an on through the day, the spring pattern continuing. The sun finally appeared and warmed the greenhouse, the first time this year. On their morning walk, Jeanie and Chris saw seven overwintering buzzards – quite a change in the migration pattern.

2007: Rain continues to be the rule – instead of snow. Mike Triplett took part in the Christmas bird count and reported that "this was wettest Christmas count we have ever done. We have had everything from over a foot of snow to temperatures at or below freezing but never a persistent drizzle like we had last Sunday morning. The birds seemed to agree with our assessment of the weather for they were few and far apart. Our group, which covered the woods and fields of Wright State University and the gravel pits by Skyborn, saw 27 species, which included a great horned owl, a Cooper's hawk, two pied-billed grebes, and a Northern mockingbird."

2008: Casey called at a quarter to three this afternoon. "There are hundreds of robins here on the front campus of the college near the Horace Mann monument," he said. "It's like a whole yard full of robins, and they keep coming in from the northwest. They're scratching in the snow, digging under leaves."

2009: Storm warning all day today, big flakes of snow coming down. When I walked into the back yard, I found the back Osage and locust trees full of hundreds of starlings, clucking and fluffing. I put birdseed out, but the flock never came down to eat. Snow fell throughout the day, gentle and soft. Tonight as I walked Bella, the flakes were so big, the streetlight cast their shadows on the drifts.

2011: Crows at 7:45 this morning.

2014: Cardinals sang steadily as I walked Bella this morning between 9:15 and 9:45. Snowdrops are now two inches high, and a few snow crocus that high, too. One Lenten rose has buds. Sun and frost, barometer 29.80. In the afternoon, Liz reported: "I have spotted bluebirds at Ellis this last week, several today and several at one of the boxes along the lane earlier this week."

2017: An ice storm sweeps across the country from the southern plains into the Middle Atlantic region.

2018: Palatka, Florida to Statesville, North Carolina: Sun and 40s throughout the drive. Snow approaching from the west, due in Ohio after midnight.

2020: From Yellow Springs to Athens, Tennessee: A mild morning, the whole eastern half of the country, except the Northeast, with above-normal temperatures. The roadside grasses and fields were northern-dull until below Lexington, Kentucky. Shirtsleeve weather in Tennessee. Clumping of wild onions, a few dandelions in bloom. From Yellow Springs, Ed Oxley reports seeing two tan moths this morning.

2021: The Christmas bird count reports the greatest diversity of birds ever, and the count of Canadian geese was 383. Today at Ellis, I have never seen so many geese, maybe 450 to 500.

2022: Jack called to tell me that his wife, Jane, saw an Eastern bluebird in the Pine Forest yesterday.

Journal

We often have an Advent Wreath at our house during December, and this year we decided to extend its vigil past solstice and Christmas to the average date of the arrival of Early Spring in our village of Yellow Springs, Ohio, February 18, a total of twelve weeks marked by twelve candles.

At the very beginning of December, the Yellow Springs sun goes down at its earliest time, 5:10 PM, and so it was always dark outside when the first candle was lit before supper at half past five. By the time the fifth candle was lit on New Year's Eve, sunset had moved to 5:20, and by January 11 to 5:30, and by the 20th to 5:40, by the 31st close to 6:00.

The sixth and seventh candles watched through the coldest part of the season, the eight and ninth saw the January Thaw, the tenth the Groundhog Day Thaw, the eleventh and twelfth the last snows of middle February.

As the number of lit candles increased, the brightness of the wreath and the brightness of the sky started to balance one another at supper time until, even when the sky was overcast on the very last day of Late Winter, the light of the twelve candles was almost superfluous, the sun setting at 6:15.

Then, even though the weather might continue to be cold, a new vigil and new measurements could begin, this time with a gauge of cut pussy willow and forsythia branches, forced crocuses, tulips and daffodils.

If you would draw closer to Nature, age with Nature. Find a portion of the raw world that is nearby. Adopt it. Your concern for the fate of Nature can be played out and developed through the degree of care you devote to this one tiny area of the whole.... No matter how small an area it may be, it creates particular harmonics that ripple across your common time and space. The degree of your sincerity of concerns draws taut the weave, creating a four-dimensional tapestry: Nature, time, space, and you.

Peter London, *Drawing Closer to Nature*

January 15th
The 15th Day of the Year

A day of thaw. Early this morning crows flew westward over the prairie, cawing in the fresh, temperate air, their voices as always filling the morning with the promise of spring.

August Derleth, *A Countryman's Journal,* January 15th

Sunrise/set: 7:55/5:34
Day's Length: 9 hours 39 minutes
Average High/Low: 34/19
Average Temperature: 26
Record High: 65 – 1932
Record Low: - 13 – 1893

The Daily Weather

Today's high temperature distribution: chances of 50s are 15 percent, of 40s ten percent, of 30s forty percent, of 20s twenty percent, of teens ten percent, for single digits five percent. Below-zero mornings come one year in ten. The sun shines on almost half the days. Rain occurs 20 percent of the time, snow 25 percent.

The Weather in the Week Ahead

After the 15th, statistics show a warming trend that brings a 35 percent chance of a high in the 40s or 50s on the 16th, and a 40 percent chance on the 20th, 23rd and 24th. The possibility of mild weather is enhanced by the approach of the fourth cold front of the month. The low-pressure trough leading that front often brings in warm southerly winds. During January's third week in 1890, the longest record-breaking thaw in Lower Midwestern history warmed temperatures into the upper 60s for three days.

On the other hand, days when the temperature does not rise above zero occur more often this week than in any other Yellow Springs week, and morning lows below zero occur more in the third week of January than in any other week of the year. The driest day of the period is the 18th, with just a 25 percent chance of showers or flurries. All the rest of the days carry about a 50 percent chance of rain or snow.

Natural Calendar

My daybooks for the third week of Yellow Springs January, the second week of the Sun in Capricorn, record snow and cold but also thaws and warmth. I look for events that contradict the winter, and in January, many of those events not only anticipate spring but also expand the definition of the month.

Details of history show striations in January days, show this time to be as porous with change as it is dense with darkness and Arctic power. Year after year, openings in the seemingly monolithic wall of winter accumulate to soften the texture and body of the month. The dendrites of those spaces make fissures in the whole that allow in light and color and sound and movement antithetical to the otherwise harsh weeks that lie so close to solstice.

Unlike the imposing storms of January, the events that redefine the passage of Capricorn to Aquarius are plain and small: the occasional appearance of flies and lady beetles indoors; sightings of opossums at night and overwintering robins and bluebirds in the day; the rare appearance of a butterfly (like Rick saw in the Glen on the 8th); the songs of the titmouse, the laughter of the nuthatch; the frequent arrival of starlings in town (their murmurations disrupted by the snow); the increasing frequency of mourning dove and cardinal mating calls; the first blossoming of aconites and snowdrops and snow crocuses.....

All of these events do not always happen in the same year, but together their radii pierce the rings of temporal space to offer precedent and promise that augment our understanding of the season. Perhaps best of all, their collective story reveals a simple and happy truth, that these dimensions are not hidden, that they have been here all along, and that they and so many others can appear and transform the meaning of our world in the blinking of an eye.

Daybook

1986: Deep Winter came two weeks early, ten days before Christmas. Now the weather is mild, and there's not much time left for snow. The cold is fragile, even in January.

1988: Cardinals sang at 11:00 a.m. Now they're quiet (1:15 p.m.).

1994: In the middle of the coldest spell in years: my thermometer said 14 below zero this morning. Now the flowering cabbages and the last of the wintering foliage are withered and prostrate. West toward Richmond, the Mad River is almost completely frozen over, the first time I've seen it so white. Geese were flying north over the highway late this afternoon. One robin seen just outside of town.

1998: To Springfield: a giant flock of crows passed over U.S. 68, heading north. Part of the January migration - or one of the many short winter shifts in place the great overwintering flocks make?

2000: In November, I noticed a great blue heron in one of the new man-made ponds near the freeway. Canadian geese were feeding on the grass beside the water and beside the restaurants being built, apparently unfazed by the heavy traffic and the construction around the supermarket. Last week, I saw the heron again at the pond, hunting, gray against the snow. The geese were there, too.

2001: Cardinal calling around 8:30 this morning. Blue jay at 10:00.

2002: Susi's snowdrops are two inches high.

2004: Liz reports seeing 50 or 60 robins along the Talus Trail in North Glen today. It's two weeks early for the first flocks, but that is a big group of robins to be overwintering.

2005: Crows calling in the west at 7:35 this morning.

2006: Honeysuckle berries are down to maybe a tenth of what they were in November, rapid berry-fall over the last two weeks of mild weather. Robins heard throughout the village, and pileated woodpeckers call from the back lot. In spite of the warm January with highs in the 30s to almost 60, no snowdrop foliage seen.

2007: The front yard flooded more than I've ever seen it. There is no way out of the yard without walking through standing water.

Bulbs continue to push up. Some daffodils at Don's are at least three inches. One spicebush along High Street has actually leafed out in the past day or two – highs in the 50s and steady rain.

2008: Bittersweet berries are almost all gone now along High Street. The fat squirrel with white feet that has come to the bird feeder this month showed up today with half a tail. Is the hawk the culprit?

2010: The first morning above freezing all year, snow melting quickly, the day soft with thaw. Cardinal at 9:00 and a cardinal and titmouse at 9:30 this morning.

2011: In the back yard, almost all the winterberries have fallen, and the honeysuckle berries are almost all down, as well. And about the cranes, Liz writes: "I had a wonderful walk around the corn field behind Ellis Pond this morning and had a double treat! First I noticed two sandhill cranes fly up from the field and first they flew west, then circled to the northeast...I could hear their clicking/ purring call, and really got a good look at their silhouettes, though from a distance. At the same time, I saw one or two red foxes playing in the corn stubble. I was too far away to visualize details, but the color and the movement were unmistakable. I was so torn about which to look at, but mostly the cranes won. For the longest time, though, the foxes stayed in good sight and then they went across the creek and into the woods. I continued my walk back to where I'd seen them, and Mattie, my dog, got very excited when we found their tracks."

2018: Home from Florida to wind and flurries, snow six inches deep throughout the yard, the deepest in a year or two.

2019: Emily writes: "On January 15th I was out in the South Glen and saw a bald eagle flying over the covered bridge at the confluence of Yellow Springs Creek and Little Miami River. One. Magestic. Special! First sighting I've ever had in Yellow Springs! I know they've been around YS, but wow, to see them in person, back nesting in Ohio, when I've really only know their successful increase in population in Minnesota and Florida, is simply breathtaking."

2020: Athens, Tennessee to Lake City, Florida: Dropping down into a completely other season marked by bright green grass, more clumping of weed growth and emerald fields below Atlanta, fleabane, white clover, black medic, Spanish needles in Lake City: an early Yellow Springs May. Comparing this trip to that of 2018, I can see the benign results of a mild December and January, the region in which hard frost had not penetrated remaining well above Florida and the Gulf itself.

2023: Two sparrow hawks and one large hawk seen on high wires during a drive to Dayton.

Journal

Sometimes the transition between Deep Winter and Late Winter carries a great thaw. One day I went out to the river in the warmth of such a thaw, when cumulus clouds sped across the sky in gusts of the southwest wind, and the water of the river shone with low, brisk waves of silvers, blues and grays.

The oaks of the far bank were black against the bright sky. Up the hill, patches of yellow Osage glowed like the flush of expanding spring buds. Below the trees, hardy green chickweed, wild onion, garlic mustard, henbit and hemlock lay akimbo across the melting snow. Crows called from beyond the road.

The river had flooded earlier in the week. Mounds and drifts of silt and sand followed the course of the flood along the paths. In the bottomland the high water had uncovered foliage of buttercups and ragwort and sweet rockets.

In the swamp, fat skunk cabbage curled above the mud, many plants open and blooming. Broken white stalks of last May's angelica crunched under my feet as I picked my way across the wetland. The rivulets that passed through the grassy bogs were full and fast. I saw small fingerlings swimming in one stream. I surprised a water strider in an eddy of a brook, beside watercress and duckweed.

Climbing to the top of the hill above me, I saw the river and its tributaries become paths of light. Then along the ridge: a patch of fog, and the brilliant curves disappeared. There was no other side to the river. The enclosure of the mist revealed both the confinement and the freedom of the valley. I lost my landmarks and my limits.

January 16th
The 16th Day of the Year

There is no season such delight can bring,
As summer, autumn, winter, and the spring.

William Browne

Sunrise/set: 7:55/5:35
Day's Length: 9 hours 40 minutes
Average High/Low: 34/18
Average Temperature: 26
Record High: 59 – 1928
Record Low: - 17 – 1977

The Daily Weather

Although normal average temperatures are the coldest of the year for the next week or two, weather history shows that there is a greater chance (20 percent) for highs today above 50 than on any other day this month (except for the 4th and the 17th), and fifteen percent of the time the highs are in the 40s. On balance, 30 percent of the afternoons bring 30s, and 25 percent bring 20s. Five percent are in the teens, another five in the single digits. Fifteen percent of the mornings are below zero. There is 20 percent chance of snow, 20 percent chance of rain, and the sun shines five days in a decade.

Natural Calendar

The Season of the Coldest Average Temperatures of the year begins on January 16 and lasts through January 28. The close of the Season of Berryfall and the first signs of the Season of Junco Migration marks this time of year; watch for those birds to form small flocks and move north for breeding. Crow Migration Season occurs in the last weeks of January, southern migrants joining the overwintering flocks, jousting for position as pairing off starts for spring mating. Opossum, Skunk and Raccoon Courting Seasons are also talking form.

Florist's Daffodil, Tulip, Crocus, and Hyacinth Season opens by the middle of January's third week: Florists and grocery stores are introducing flowering spring bulbs, either potted or as cut flowers. Asian Ladybug Emerging Season calls out ladybugs onto sunny windowsills this time of the month. Housefly Emerging Season often sometimes accompanies the appearance of the less intrusive ladybeetles. Both of those insect varieties are especially partial to the Season of the January Thaw, which typically warms several days between January 17 and 26. January 21 is the first day of the Season of the Possibility of 70-Degree highs in the Lower Midwest, a season that lasts through December 6.

Daybook

1988: The river is frozen all the way across at Sycamore Hole. But I saw a bluebird this afternoon.

1989: A cardinal sang at 8:30 and at 11:00. In this mild winter, they are more active than I remember. Pussy willows are opening now, maybe a fourth of the catkins showing. In the late afternoon, starlings are cackling and whistling by Sycamore Hole. Only a few goldenrod seeds noticed hanging on.

1991: A cardinal sang at 7:55 a.m. That's the earliest I've heard them this time of year. When they call a half an hour earlier, Deep Winter will have shifted to Late Winter.

1993: Sparrows fighting: 8:45 a.m. Cardinal singing at 9:10, a long song, but more up and down, more simply cadenced than the mating song to come in two weeks; short song burst at about 11:00, then quiet the rest of the day. The sun was out three hours straight for the first time this year. Jeanie said that she saw a raccoon crossing the school ground yesterday afternoon. Are the opossums moving too?

1996: Wearing my father's wool jacket, my mother's Irish shawl around my legs, I sit in the greenhouse, and listen to the High Street wind and watch the sun come over my neighbor's roof through the morning flurries, behind winter tomatoes and red geraniums, impatiens and pansy sprouts.

2000: 8:00 a.m. Squirrels chasing each other in the back mulberry tree. On the way to church, I heard crows, sparrows, starlings, a tufted titmouse all calling in the warm south winds. Flies in the greenhouse today.

2008: Crows at 7:44 this morning, a cardinal heard on my alley walk about 9:30. Greg called about 4:45 this evening, said he had seen a large flock of robins over by the college library yesterday and that now there were dozens of robins in his back yard. I walked over with Bella and saw a sizeable flock in the trees there, some of them in the gutters of the house next to Greg's house, some on the driveway, some across the street.

2009: Minus 13 degrees this morning, and the hot water pipe to the bathroom is frozen. But the pond waterfall is still running, the water open, thanks to the heater, and a tufted titmouse is singing over toward Dayton Street.

2011: Crows at 7:23 this morning, the earliest I've heard them all year.

2012: A thaw underway after only two days below freezing. Crows and a flock of about a dozen black buzzards feeding on a deer carcass along Dayton-Yellow Springs Road this morning. At the quarry, all of the shallow ponds were still frozen over, and Jeff and I walked across several of them. At home, two pots of greenhouse tomatoes, one of datura, and a flat of geraniums planted under a shop light in the attic.

2014: Clear, bright moon and crows at 7:35 this morning.

2017: Days of intermittent rain; crows calling when I cam out of the house at 7:40 this morning; five roadkills counted on the way to Xenia this morning, opossums and raccoon; a cardinal sang as I walked home from Jill's at 10:30. In the dooryard garden, I found the first Lenten rose bud, then another one in the south garden. Jane reported: "Saw a large flock of robins in John Bryan Park." The coldest average temperatures of the year occur between today and the end of the month, but the next ten days are expected to be in the 40s and 50s.

2019: Blue jay bell call at about 10:30 this morning and then around noon, sparrows, doves cardinals, chickadees feeding heavily throughout the day, snow eight-inches deep across the yard. Ellis Pond has a thin coating of ice, and the geese have left the area.

2020: Driving from Lake City, Florida to Sarasota. Sun and high 70s. From Leslie in Yellow Springs, her report for the past week: "More CARDINALS and more GRAY SQUIRRELS (peaked) this week, squirrels unusual high energy with CHASING and JUMP-FIGHTING on one day, first OSAGE ORANGE FRUIT torn apart and eaten, a song sparrow quietly sings its spring song 2x, a PILEATED and a FLICKER each visited feeding area twice, we identified species of WOODPECKER that is INTERMEDIATE in SIZE between a downy and a hairy and confirmed it is a DOWNY, 2 mourning doves seen just once this week, and first DAFFODIL green shoots which are poking up 2" high in the brick planter attached to the front of our house. In addition to the above-mentioned sightings, we also have blue jays (1-4) goldfinches (1-7), chickadees (1-3), titmice (1-3, plus calling), a white-breasted nuthatch (see just 1 each day), juncos (1-7), Carolina wren (just 1, plus calls), 5 species woodpeckers including red-bellied (1 or 2 = male and female), hairy (ocasionally see just one male); red-shouldered hawk calls, Cooper's hawk, turkey vultures, Canada geese, opossum."

2021: A walk with Ranger, 7:45 this morning, light snow, sun and jagged clouds, crows, robins, cardinals, and the clear "sweet-ee" note of the black-capped chickadee around the house and in the alley. A robin was hopping down the High Street sidewalk when I walked home from Jill's at noon.

On earth and only on earth are sunset glow, green leaf, and eyes to see them. Here is all we know of reality, all-sufficient to our destiny, our thoughts and passions.

Donald Culross Peatti

January 17th
The 17th Day of the Year

It is the time of the year when the foxes seek their mates. The wood stirs; there is hardly a night that we do not overhear some odd living sound or uneasy cry. The clock of the stars has struck, and life has awakened in the cold and has turned and has heard

Henry Beston, *Northern Farm*

Sunrise/set: 7:54/5:36
Day's Length: 9 hours 42 minutes
Average High/Low: 34/18
Average Temperature: 26
Record High: 63 – 1952
Record Low: - 21 – 1977

The Daily Weather

Highs above 50 can occur 20 percent of the time on this date, and 40s another 20 percent. Thirties are recorded 30 percent of the afternoons, and 20s on 25 percent. Highs only in the single digits come one year in 20. Fifteen percent of the time, morning lows fall below zero, and five percent of the time, the high itself does not get above zero. The sky is completely overcast half the years on this date. Rain falls 30 percent of the time, snow another 30 percent.

Natural Calendar

The year seems to pause now, frozen in the middle of Deep Winter, but natural history and our own mind of spring continue to be the sum of our observations. Since there is no limit to what a person might watch and record, stasis is only in the eye of the beholder.

When the snow melts, the landscape appears part Early Spring, part Late Fall, the grass greening in sheltered corners, the fallen leaves darkening in decay. Osage fruits have become speckled with age, many of them shredded by squirrels and raccoons. Coralberries are becoming paler, bittersweet pods almost all fallen, red winterberries and small fruits of the decorative pear trees lie scattered all over the ground.

Purple deadnettle has expanded into mounds. Pussy willows have cracked a little more, and multiflora rose buds look ready to open. Snowdrops and crocuses have started to push up through the mulch, even under the snow.

Many years, bird sightings and sounds increase in and around the village near January 17. Canadian geese often gather in great flocks on nearby fields. Crows and cardinals sing near 7:30 in the morning. Sandhill cranes continue their retreat before winter storms. Great blue herons sometimes migrate. Robins and bluebirds, overwintering or arriving early, grace the promise of spring.

Daybook

1985: 5:16 p.m., large flock of geese flying south over Xenia Avenue.

1987: Cardinals heard around 10:00 this morning. Geese flew over the east end of town just before sunset. Purple deadnettle remains unhurt by the cold along the south wall.

1990: A cardinal sang at 7:40 a.m. Are they starting their spring songs early in this record warm January?

1993: Despite the cold so far, hyacinths in the south garden have been up maybe half an inch for the past week. Coming back from the Springfield fairgrounds, I saw an opossum by the side of the road, sign of winter breaking. In the greenhouse, one mother-in-law's tongue has opened.

1994: Heavy snow and below-zero cold have shut Ohio airports, highways, schools. An eight-inch cover of snow throughout the back yard. But Marcie Rogers reported seeing a small flock of bluebirds in the Glen.

1996: Blue jays and cardinals calling at 10:30 this morning. Birds flocking again as the thaw builds; a few days ago in the snow and wind, there was nothing flying. In the greenhouse, the last Christmas cactus flower has wilted.

2002: Driving to Columbus, I saw a flock of maybe three-dozen great blue herons flying high into the northwest wind.

2004: Greg calls, reports a yellow-bellied sapsucker in a box elder tree by the west edge of his yard.

2006: Sparrows chatter in the bamboo when I walk Bella near sunrise. No cardinals heard for a week or so.

2010: The thaw continues, the pond ice slowly being absorbed into the dark water. All the small fishes are visible now for the first time since the early part of the month. Crows at 7:35 this morning, a cardinal singing at 8:07, starlings at the feeders for the past few days, geese flying over at about 11:00 and again at 2:30.

2011: Thaw beginning, highs in the 30s, rain tomorrow. When I was out about noon, a titmouse was singing steadily.

2012: High in the 50s today, gusty south winds and rain in the morning, the wind direction switching to the west then north in the afternoon. In the east garden, stonecrop foliage has come up in the past few days, and the snowdrops are now about two inches, the daffodils about the same - and more of them appearing, clear progress during the past week. Along the south edge of the yard, two of the hellebore plants have budded.

2013: Ruby reports from West College Street that "a huge flock of goldfinches and pine siskins flew in together this morning."

2014: Ed Oxley states he saw "thousands" of Canadian geese at a large quarry pond north of town. Southwestern Ohio is not on any migration route that I can find. This flock was presumably a great assembly of permanent residents. (Yellow Springs is well within their year-round habitat.)

2015: Crows at 8:00 this morning. In the thaw of the past three days, a cluster of the front garden's daffodils pushed up two inches, snowdrops came through the mulch (white tips visible), and wisps of wild onion were growing up around them. By the back porch, thin foliage of snow crocus up a couple of inches. This afternoon, across from Ellis Pond, hundreds of Canadian geese were feeding in the fields.

2016: Walking home from Jill's at 9:15 this morning: gray and flurries, a robin chirped down Highs Street, a cardinal was singing. At 10:30, Dennie Eagleton called to say she had just seen a large pod of maybe four-dozen sandhill cranes flying south over Hustead Road toward Ellis Pond and the village. Deep cold spreading south after the snow: Like the pods of January 3 and 10, these birds were flying ahead of the storm to come.

2018: Walking home from Jill's on icy roads (almost hit by a car), I heard a robin whinny over near Davis Street, and a woodpecker was working nearby.

2021: Cloudy, flurries, 33 degrees, full cardinal song at 7:35 this morning, crows at 7:40.

2022: Full moon. Second snow of the season. A major winter storm has struck the Southeast and the East, just missing eastern Ohio.

Walking as enabling sight and thought rather than encouraging retreat and escape; paths as offering not only means of traversing space, but also ways of feeling, being and knowing.

Robert Macfarlane

***January 18th**
The 18th Day of the Year*

*And then with the thaw comes up the sudden rush
Of growth that waited only on this hour,
On this disclosure of the life beneath.*

Vita Sackville-West, *The Garden*

Sunrise/set: 7:54/5:38
Day's Length: 9 hours 44 minutes
Average High/Low: 34/18
Average Temperature: 26
Record High: 67 – 1927
Record Low: - 25 – 1994

The Daily Weather

Highs warm to the 60s once every two decades, find the 50s once in a decade, reach the 40s twenty percent of the time, the 30s twenty-five percent of the time, the 20s fifteen percent, the teens 15 percent, single digits five percent, and never even reach zero five percent of the time. The sun breaks through the clouds half of all the days. Below-zero lows occur three years in 20. Rain falls 15 percent of the years, snow ten percent.

Natural Calendar

Although the United States lies in the middle of its most frigid time of the entire year, the possibility of mild conditions is enhanced by the incursion of powerful southerly winds from the Gulf of Mexico. The resulting turbulence often creates the "January Thaw," a brief space during which much milder temperatures and an increased likelihood of blizzards, thunderstorms, tornados and flooding occur.

In milder years, frost seeding typically begins at this time of the witner. Red clover is broadcast in the fields, and grass seed is scattered over bare spots on the lawn. Bedding plants such as geraniums, coleus, carnations, petunias, and snapdragons are started under lights in flats. Cold-weather broccoli, kale, collards, cabbage and celery are seeded for setting out eight to twelve weeks from now.

The Stars

Orion is the nighttime clock of winter, his hands telling high noon in the center of the southern sky as January and the cold deepen. By spring equinox, he will have slipped into the far west in the evening, rising near dawn, his Dog Star, Sirius, prophesying the Dog Days of July.

Daybook

1986: I've seen three opossums killed on the back roads so far this January, the earliest I've noticed them get hit. Late Winter always follows the possums.

1989: South to Tennessee: The grass is definitely greener 70 miles south of Yellow Springs in Cincinnati, then stable for the next 100 miles, then increases in brightness about 180 miles south of home, half an hour below Lexington.

1991: Possum killed last night along Grinnell.

1992: First fly of the year seen in the back yard basking on the south wall.

1993: Looking over the daybook notations, it seems clear that the opossums in '86 and '92, and the fly emerging last year were significant. And maybe the cardinal's song at 7:55 on January 16th, and the pussy willows opening then, too, spring's motion a matter of the first pieces of the innumerable pieces to come.

1999: On January 1, after an unusually warm autumn, the sun rose hazy through altostratus, foretelling a bitter two-week storm that brought more than a foot of snow to Yellow Springs, rain changing to ice, and below-zero temperatures, school closings, cabin fever. Days of digging out and sliding, of hibernation, ordering seeds, walking downtown for food.

On the 16th, it was over. The temperature climbed into the upper 40s. The cardinals were singing by 9:00 a.m. The great gray stratus banks of the storm came apart by mid-morning. Under the sudden blue sky, trees dropped their snowmelt, water pattering to the ground in the sun. The wind picked up, pushing off more ice to shatter onto the streets, bringing down twigs and branches.

The barometer dropped throughout the 17th, and the crows were up by 7:30 in the morning, the sparrows were loud, the cardinals calling. At Mills Lawn, a giant pileated woodpecker worked the tall hickory, sending out an abbreviated spring song. At Jacoby, the heavy crust of the glazed snow was giving in, and the brooks were showing through the ice where cowslips bloom in April. Some of the spring beds were bright green with chickweed, cress, and grass, unhurt by the terrible cold of the past two weeks.

The blue jays were never too far away, watching and talking. Kingfishers chattered up and down the opening waterway. Ducks were feeding. I walked out to the middle of the swamp and counted skunk cabbage, twelve heads showing. On one log, moss was growing, sending out its flower heads.

By the middle of the afternoon, the thaw was quieting. The sky filled again with clouds, and rain started to fall. By early night, the first thunderstorm of the year clashed with the next cold front approaching, but it was a gentle front, carrying bluster, but little else. By dawn, most of the snow had disappeared, and the wind blew hard all day from the southwest.

2008: The first starlings of the year appeared in the yard today, and one robin. Yesterday on the way to Wilmington around four o'clock, I noticed two large flocks of starlings – and similar flocks have not been common since late fall. Have this week's robins and starlings been driven ahead of the deep cold wave due to arrive tomorrow? Or are these flocks simply arriving on time and I haven't noticed before? A black wooly bear caterpillar taken off of one of the pieces of firewood this evening, put outside on the back porch.

2010: The first snowdrop and snow crocus tips visible as the snow melts in the east garden.

2011: More melting underway, light rain. Crows at 7:41 this morning. Birds feeding sporadically, squirrels more active around the feeders.

2018: Thaw beginning today after snow and several days of deep cold, the second major thaw of this January. I resumed feeding the birds after a break of twelve days. It didn't take long for the chickadees, sparrows, blue jays, cardinals and even starlings (the first time I've seen them in the yard this year) to find the food. In the afternoon, a grackle joined the feeding, and a robin came to the fountain, drank and drank. Then I noticed that the house wren had joined the others in the suet cage and on the ground. This evening, the first fly of the year was buzzing around me as I read in the living room.

2019: Louise reports a small flock of bluebirds on Polecat Road near Ellis Pond. When I arrived at Jill's this morning, I watched two red-tailed hawks playing in randori in the high maples. Cardinals heard off and on today. Near Ellis, winterberry fruits were scattered along the bike path. An outburst from the flock of geese nearby lasted a few minutes, then silence.

2020: Sarasota, Florida: Complete semi-tropical habitat, no sign of Ohio winter. Looking back over today's Yellow Springs daybook, I see how all the notes reach south, look forward. The notations from the cold, Midwestern years are fragments of longing as well as projections, reachings toward, visualizing, collecting pieces of the puzzle of spring knowing that the completion is only a matter of distance or circumstance or decision, realizing that the details of January – such as cardinal song or the sighting of bluebirds or the gathering of geese or the appearance of snowdrop tips pushing through the mulch – are almost artificial constructs, a toying with promises and signs, the fulfillment of which already exists only a few hundred miles away. And yet, for all those years, that fulfillment felt so achingly, impossibly distant.

I am reminded of the time I was stationed at Fort Clayton in Panama half a century ago, a trip to Bogota, Colombia, in the Andes surprised me with the change in altitude and temperature, showed me that the thick, moist air of the tropics was simply downhill from the sharp chill of the mountains. And when I visited Neysa in Italy in 2010 and we drove up the foothills of the

Apennines from May back into April to buy cheese from shepherds, I felt the same sense of dislocation, felt again the contradiction of expectations, the confusion from space forming warps in my consciousness, revealing to me once again the unreliability of perspective and the illusion of permanence.

2021: Thirty degrees and light sleet: cardinals began to sing in the Phillips Street alley at exactly 7:33 this morning.

The almanac of time hangs in the brain:
The seasons numbered, by the inward sun....

Dylan Thomas

January 19th
The 19th Day of the Year

Of all aspects of life, nature alone offered the only constant, the only permanence – even though the seasonal changes symbolized the inevitable changes which must come to me in my own seasons.

August Derleth

Sunrise/set: 7:53/5:39
Day's Length: 9 hours 46 minutes
Average High/Low: 34/18
Average Temperature: 26
Record High: 68 – 1907
Record Low: - 25 – 1994

The Daily Weather
The fifth January cold front, often followed by a longer period (up to four or five days, instead of only two) of milder weather, arrives soon. Today and tomorrow are the last two days of the month on which there is a 20 percent chance of a morning below zero. The next time chances get so high will be the 6th of February. Highs remain only in the teens or below 20 percent of the time, are in the 20s another ten percent, and in the 30s fifty percent. Warmer 40s occur the remaining 20 percent. Precipitation comes four years in ten on this date, and the sun shines at least a little six years in ten.

Natural Calendar
Now as the day lengthens, the advance of spring quickens. Crows know all about the expanding daylight. Their migration cycle typically starts at the early edge of the night's retreat. Junco movement begins in mid-January, too, just as the sun comes into Aquarius.

This is also the week opossums and raccoons become more active, and they appear at night along the backroads. Once you sight these small mammals, then you know for sure late winter is on the way. Skunk cabbage is up in the swamps, blackened by the cold but still strong. Watercress holds in the streams. Where the ground is not frozen, new mint grows under the protection of a southern hedge or wall. In the pastures, basal leaves of thistles and mullein are deep green beneath the snow. In town, winter-blooming hellebores and Chinese witch hazels blossom in the warmest microclimates.

As the thaws move north from Kentucky, remnants of the past year no longer point back to October. On the hillsides, the springs are clear and the vegetation bright. New chickweed covers parts of the bottomland. Basal foliage of sweet rocket and leafcup is lush and tall, waiting for April and May.

As you walk through the wetlands in the January Thaw, small, pale moths may follow you, and you may see crayfish crawling along through the shallow water.

In the greenhouse, jade tree flowers have come to the end of their cycle, the white petals rusting. In the dooryards, snowdrops have come up, many with their pale white bud-like tips showing.

Daybook

1984: Juncos feeding along Wilberforce-Clifton Road, the first sign of their migration.

1985: Flocks of juncos feeding along Wilberforce-Clifton. Seven inches of snow on the ground, a storm moving in. The rush of wind all day, sun in and out. The seed shells of the backyard locust came loose in the wind, clutter the snow.

1989: On the way through South Carolina: The first flower seen in bloom, a roadside sow thistle. Buzzards were circling, and the first trees were definitely in bloom 60 miles north of Savanna. A daffodil was budding at the Georgia line. Some black medic and white clover, red clover and dandelions were in full bloom, too, fifty days away from South Glen. Thistles had thick stalks, boot high, June size. Wild onions were as tall as in April in Yellow Springs. Throughout the cities, the tree line was pink with flowers. Just past the Florida state line, we saw a flock of robins flying north along the coast. More sow thistles were completely open, along with dock, hairy chickweed and bittercress.

1990: Cardinal singing by 8:00 a.m.

1993: Mother-of-millions still full bloom in the greenhouse. Janet Hackett says that her snowdrops are up and budded. Nothing here in the south garden.

1994: Record 25 degrees below zero this morning in Yellow Springs. Snow crystals, fragments of condensed moisture, float through the sun like miniature fireflies, bringing the air into motion with the appearance of organic life.

1995: Rain and mild. I heard a cardinal singing in the dark when I let the dog out this morning at 7:15. The predawn song has begun early, maybe encouraged by this warm winter.

1996: An opossum killed on Grinnell Road last night, on the move after yesterday's deep thaw.

1998: In the pond, wild iris spears that braved weeks of ice stand strong around the broken strands of lizard's tail. As the bamboo in my south garden recovers from the weight of the snow, it shows sweet rockets, ground ivy, great mullein, celandine, wild lettuce, dock, sweet Williams and lamb's ear waiting for April and May.

2005: Two small flocks of crows seen today. I've been hearing them more in the mornings, too. They are getting restless right on time.

2007: The first half of January was warm; now comes the cold. The snowdrops stand stiff on the frozen ground. In the woods, the new foliage that came out during five weeks of mild weather has wilted. At our bird feeders, more songbirds are here today, fewer sparrows. A mouse has started visiting the lower drawer in the stove.

2008: Deep cold moving in on the north wind today. Starlings and at least one robin still around in the south shrubbery this morning. By early afternoon, the starlings found the bird feeder and the suet in the east garden.

2009: A short thaw after the below-zero temperatures, then a return of moderate cold. About five inches of snow on the ground. No change noted in the birds or branches. A new animal in the attic took the peanut butter bait I set out yesterday.

2010: Crows around 8:00, a cardinal at 9:00 this morning. Mild weather continues.

2011: Crows at 7:44 this morning.

2013: The wind blows hard today, the sky clear and the sun warm, temperature getting up into the low 50s this afternoon. In the north garden, I have a handful of daffodils budded, one almost completely open, one showing a lot of color. In two days, the low is expected to fall into the single digits, so I may cut off the flowers and bring them in. All around the yard, in addition to the surge in the daffodils, there has been a strong growth of snow crocus and snowdrops, the warm autumn having accelerated so many things beyond what I expected.

2015: A cardinal was calling in the distance when I went out at 9:20 this morning. Sun and in the 20s. A large flock of Canadian geese, maybe a hundred or more passed over Yellow Springs heading south this afternoon.

2016: Cold, 5 degrees, clear: Crows at 7:42 a.m.

2018: Walking through the neighborhood with Jill, I noticed sweet gum seedpods and small pear fruits scattered in the melting snow.

2019: Small flocks of starlings noticed in town, storm wind gusting, light rain and flurries. Leslie reports a flock of 38 house and gold finches and 26 starlings at her feeders.

2021: Clear and crisp this morning. The first cardinal sang at 7:26. This afternoon when Jill and I were walking back from Talus Drive, we looked up and saw a murmuration of birds, smaller than starlings, swooping and swooping far overhead, circling the waxing moon, the sun glinting on their feathers.

John Bleakelock wrote a note about pollination and bees: "Back in the '70s: Pip McCaslin, Chris Moore, and I were devotees of Euell Gibbons. We were always trying to make our own wine from elder-blow (the flowers), or the berries. In those days, the umbels had almost universal pollination--hardly a barren ovary to be seen. They were full, heavy bunches-- quick and easy to obtain a bountiful harvest. Now, I notice elderberries have about a 5% successful pollination rate. Really, the rate is the *opposite* of what it used to be. Because we were so intimately involved in gathering them, over a period of 3 years, that is a memory I have complete confidence in."

When I asked him about making wine with elderberries, he replied, "not nearly enough berries. All stems these days. And I don't really like the flavor."

2022: A brief, one-day January thaw today, with a high of 47, melting snow, woodpeckers tapping across the street and in the woods behind my yard.

2023: The geese were out on the pond today, the open water deep blue like the sky, between 200 and 300 geese drifting across the water, bright black and white.

Journal

The ice on the river had broken up, and the great thaw was underway. My bulldog, Buttercup, and I followed the paths up and along the hills. It was late in the afternoon. The sky had been gray all day, now was darker with storm clouds. We walked through flurries, sometimes a shower of sleet. At first, the noise from the cars along the road intruded on our privacy, but as we moved further back into the woods, the rush of the flooding river and the rising wind swallowed up highway sounds.

Much of the snow of the past week had melted. The land was a patchy gray and black, brown and deep green. Even after the recent record-low temperatures, chickweed was still bright, and garlic mustard, aster, henbit, wild strawberry, ground ivy, and sweet rocket leaves pushed out through the ice.

Deer tracks were visible in what was left of the snow. They were the only tracks I saw. Buttercup seemed not to notice them, preferred to romp and frisk, bite at sticks, climb over the stumps of fallen trees.

The water was as high as I'd ever seen it. Usually clear and shallow, it was deep and fast and full of mud after two days of rain and melting snow. Buttercup was nervous at its power, walked to the riverbank, then scampered back to me shaking, excited and afraid.

I walked with her, thinking how low this same river had been in the drought of 1988, how it had seemed so vulnerable and ephemeral then, how the fish had gathered in the deeper pools, huddled together against the increasing warmth and stagnation of the current and the mysterious withdrawal of the earth's life force.

Today, there was none of that old fragility, and Wendell Berry's poem on the second coming of the wilderness ran through my mind. I was standing, I imagined, in front of what Berry called "a resurrection of the wild."

This flood was like a sudden, sweeping memory of a massive waterway 15,000 years ago when humans were just beginning to hunt in the newly-formed hills and when this excess would have been only low tide of that ancient global warming, the collapse of the Ice Age filling the hollows with snowmelt.

I wondered if the flood might also be a prophesy of this place 15,000 years from now, the valley filling again in the long storms of another climate, the river rising to cleanse the land of all our impurities, purging itself of our waste. Our words and structures would have disappeared by then, those people who might remain alive having no more knowledge of us than I of the fur-clad hunters and their wolf-dogs who tracked the ancestors of today's deer, men and women who stood in this same place as Buttercup and I and who wondered what might someday come to pass.

January 20th
The 20th Day of the Year

I cherish
the comfort of crows:
waking over High Street
at 7:42 in the morning
or about that time in late January
every year, even though it seems
time moves straight ahead
and that it pulls me with it into death.
It's not as though the crows can save me
Or will take me out of line,
But their stability soothes me:
everything else swept away,
they are a radius of constancy
piercing the linear Gregorian undertow
that drags me out to sleep,
their momentary calls perennial,
prophesies I wish I could believe.

bf

Sunrise/set: 7:53/5:40
Day's Length: 9 hours 47 minutes
Average High/Low: 34/18
Average Temperature: 26
Record High: 69 – 1906
Record Low: - 24 – 1985

The Daily Weather

On this date in my weather records, a high in the 50s occurs five percent of the time, and mild 40s come on 40 percent of the afternoons. Cooler 30s are recorded 25 percent of the days, with the remaining 30 percent in the 20s or below. Chances of snow today are 40 percent, of sun 50 percent.

The foliage of the oakleaf hydrangea has often fallen by this point in the year. The Osage fruits have turned deep red-brown. Azalea leaves curl and darken. The berries of the euonymus are coming away from their decaying, once protective sepals. Junco gathering for migration north begins, just as the sun comes into Aquarius.

The Sun

The Sun enters its astrological sign of Aquarius on or about the 20th, foreshadowing Late Winter.

Daybook

1989: Jacksonville, Florida in the middle of Middle Spring: Elderberries and azaleas blooming. Some sugar maples half to fully leafed. A flock of robins seen at 4:00 p.m., beds of pansies blooming. Calves in the fields. My daughter, Jeni, found a newborn turtle last week in the pond by her apartment.

1990: First crocus up under the peach tree. Cardinals - sporadic song.

1991: Birds active this morning, cardinal heard off and on between 8:00 and 9:00, crows flying over. An average January so far, and perennials show slight growth.

1992: Seven pots of wandering Jews hang against the greenhouse windows, safe from the wind on the other side. My tomatoes hold motionless to their trellises. The violet hibiscus bloom and fall without a sound, are replenished every day. The cacti below them neither increase in size nor die back. Winter zinnias have retained their color and shape for the past month.

I have a journal of the greenhouse and the outside cycles. I keep a planting and nature log, and I carefully measure the natural progress of year. But now I'm losing interest in the records, am turning to plants that change the least. I want things to stay the way they are. I don't care if equinox comes. I wish winter would never end. I'm comfortable with its limits. I'm content with the finite number of species in the ten by thirty foot greenhouse.

I know the static world better than I will ever know the

new emerging world. Since the end of October, I've kept this season stable and warm, arbitrarily favored coleus over calendulas, jade trees over geraniums, angel wing begonias over marigolds. Even the white flies and the mealy bugs contributed to equilibrium, their hunger offsetting growth.

At night I sit by the immutable, invulnerable leaves. I identify with them, hide with them behind this glass south wall, feel our alliance and our common purpose. No April birds are singing. There are no fireflies or crickets to mark the mark the passage of the year and of our lives, no signs that any of this could ever end.

2005: As the cold deepens, it pushes me to withdraw from people even more than I usually do. But then I struggle with loneliness, and I ruminate about solitude and isolation. The former is contained and confident; the latter is needy and implies that separation is insufficiency. Solitude implies context and self-reliance and safety. To break isolation, I struggle to sever the ties of my insecurities and doubts, enemies of serenity. I try to allow approval and dependency and worry to fall away behind me. In solitude, I still keep the companionship of memory and affection. I hold to the good of the past. I carry gratitude and love with me into my winter retreat, invite them to support the walls of my seclusion. Then the sun and the thaws become stronger, and none of this seems to matter.

2006: After a very mild January, I took inventory at the beginning of Late Winter. Snowdrops, some daffodils and hyacinths were up about an inch around the yard. Snow crocus were two inches above the mulch, ready to bud. Purple deadnettle, bittercress and chickweed were slowly spreading across the garden.

I found one new wild strawberry leaf, one new waterleaf sprout. There was fresh growth on the Japanese honeysuckle, leaves dark violet, venturing out from the axils of their woody vines. A few red nubs of peonies had appeared.

The foliage of the oak-leaf hydrangea had fallen in the past two weeks. The Osage fruits had turned deep red-brown. The berries of the euonymus were falling from their decaying, once protective sepals. No pussy willow catkins were open yet; I cut a branch and brought it indoors, set it in a vase of warm water.

I walked beyond the Covered Bridge late in the afternoon with Bella, our border-collie-spaniel. The temperature was almost 60 degrees, the river high. Garlic mustard was lush on the hillsides. In protected hollows, cushions of chickweed were deep March green.

Black walnut hulls were dark and collapsing, fell away at the touch of my heel. Only a few box elder seeds were hanging from their branches, thinning now like the honeysuckle berries. Young poison hemlock was feathery and spreading. New ragwort and sweet rocket leaves were pushing up. Cautious skunk cabbage spears were just barely visible.

Even though I was a little disappointed at the slow progress of the plants during such a warm, month-long thaw, Bella had no reservations about the state of the landscape. A far better observer than I, she took a different inventory, and she ran and ran for joy once we reached the bright meadows below the Vale.

2008: The coldest morning of the year so far, the low at one degree above zero. A large flock of starlings has settled in our block, feeding in the grass, warming themselves on the chimney tops.

2009: The trees and forsythia are frosted this morning, and accented with a light dust of snow. Starlings whistle in the distance, and a robin is chirping near the north garden. A pair of doves has started coming to the back bird feeder this past week.

2010: Crows at 7:30 this morning, just as the snow moves in from the west. Titmouse heard at about 10:00, and Judy sends a message at the same time from Goshen, Indiana, a titmouse there, too.

2012: Finally a few days of deeper cold. At the bird feeder, five female cardinals and two males. Two starlings feeding with them, but no cardinal calls yet these mornings. Sleet in the evening.

2013: Cold front moving in, single digits expected tomorrow. First crows at 7:37 this morning.

2014: Storm due tonight, then very cold in the single digits. Crows at 7:50 this morning.

2015: Three flocks of geese, each at least thirty birds, seen as I drove to and from Xenia this morning. I begin to wonder about the winter movement of geese: Is it because they are searching for open water, or because of the thaw of the last three days (and the melting of ice on ponds), or both? At Kathy's this afternoon, flies were emerging from somewhere in the walls, buzzing against her south windows, and an Asian ladybeetle was crawling up and down the window glass beside them. At the fen along Fairground Road, we followed the boardwalk, talking about wildflowers, bird watching and death.

2016: In the cold and snow at 8:30 this morning, a peeping robin, then crows beyond Stafford Street. Yesterday, I saw that Ellis Pond had frozen over; the geese were all huddled together on the other side of the road, hundreds of them, many heads tucked into their wings.

2017: The news reports that 2016 was the world's warmest year on record, the third year in a row. At Jill's this afternoon, an Asian ladybeetle was wandering across the inside glass on her back door. Raking in the yard, I uncovered daffodils and hyacinths at least an inch tall underneath the leaves.

2018: Two deer at the bird feeder this morning around 8:00. Two more flies have appeared in the house.

2019: Deep cold below zero, perigee and full moon, clear and bright.

2022: After a short thaw, sun and cold once again.

> *I will confront these shows of the day and night,*
> *I will know if I am to be less than they,*
> *I will see if I am not as majestic as they.*

Walt Whitman

Blest, who can unconcern'dly find
Hours, days, and years steal soft away
In health of body, peace of mind,
Quiet day by day.

Alexander Pope

Sunrise/set: 7:52/5:41
Day's Length: 9 hours 49 minutes
Average High/Low: 34/18
Average Temperature: 26
Record High: 75 – 1906
Record Low: - 20 – 1984

The Daily Weather

Today's high temperature distribution: Fifteen percent chance of 50s or higher, 15 percent of 40s, forty percent chance of 30s, twenty percent of 20s, ten percent of teens or single digits. Half the days bring some sunshine; rain falls twice in a decade on this date, snow just a bit more often. Below-zero mornings occur 20 percent of the time.

Natural Calendar

The brisk pace of winter high pressure systems often grows sluggish and stalls between the 21st and the 26th, causing a major warm-up (the January thaw). Snowfall is normally the lightest of any other week this month; highs often shoot up above 50, and a day in the 70s suddenly becomes possible (at least once or twice in a century). A thunderstorm even occurs ten percent of all the years.

When the snow melts, fresh growth emerges on the Japanese honeysuckle, leaves dark violet, venturing out from the axils of their woody vines. In the garden, a few red nubs of peonies appear. Garlic mustard is lush on the hillsides. In the swamps, young poison hemlock is feathery and spreading, watercress bright in the springs of the talus slopes. New ragwort and sweet rocket leaves push up.

Daybook

1989: Heading home north from Jacksonville, Florida: Few trees in bloom above Macon, almost no signs of spring north of Atlanta (about 350 miles north of Florida). The grass beside the freeway becomes uniformly brown, but occasional tufts of wild onions are green. At a rest stop above Chattanooga, moss is long on an old log, the only indication I'm in the South. In northern and middle Tennessee: rolling fields of bright green wheat. Then winter returns from Kentucky into the Ohio Valley.

1990: After three weeks of mild weather, the perennials are coming back, fresh poppy leaves, new pyrethrums and wrinkled lemon verbena.

1991: South Glen, an inch or two of snow: The river is high but clear, steel blue in the partly sunny afternoon. Possible sighting of a bluebird. A cardinal sang about 4:00 p.m. At the bird feeder, I saw the only song sparrow so far this season.

1996: A cardinal was singing at 8:00 this morning. Blue jays were calling in the yard. The year is moving in spite of all the cold and snow.

1998: Sparrows singing at about five this evening along Xenia Avenue.

2000: Giant flock of geese seen over Springfield just before class about 12:45 p.m.

2001: Skunk killed along Dayton-Yellow Springs Road west of the village.

2006: Suzanne Patterson wrote me: "Between 3:00 and 4:00 p. m. I saw at least four Eastern Bluebirds in the South Glen close to the Butterfly Meadow area. Spectacular show."

2008: In the alley, two male cardinals seemed to be jockeying for position (maybe territory) in one of the trees.

2009: Only a handful of honeysuckle berries are left on the front bush.

2010: More snowdrops emerging in the east garden, the January thaw building to peak on schedule, on the 23rd and 24th.

2011: Coldest low so far this year, just one degree above zero, five inches of new snow on the ground. Crows at 7:45 again this morning. Titmice and cardinals sang as I shoveled snow. Starlings joined the sparrows at the bird feeders in the early afternoon. From the edge of town, Mary Sue writes about the pair of sandhill cranes that she found in December: "A month and counting since the first sighting and they are still here this frigid morning. Following the same routine."

2012: First crows heard at 7:30 a.m. The first tomato plant pushed up through the soil last night in the greenhouse. I planted them with the geraniums (now fourteen sprouts) on the 16th.

2013: As the cold moved in and temperatures dropped below freezing, I went out and cut five daffodil stems, most of them about four or five inches long. One of the flowers had been trying to open all the way for days; the others were still tightly budded. The stems were frozen all the way through, but I put them in water to see how they would do.

2014: Crows at 7:32 this morning, deep cold. The news reports that Lake Erie has frozen over, greatly reducing the lake-effect snow.

2015: Late morning: As I walked Bella around the block, a cardinal sang in the distance almost the whole way. When I talked to Casey in the afternoon, he said that he had been seeing flocks of geese flying "all over the place," supporting my observations of the past week. He thought it was a little unusual, too.

2016: The government reports that 2015 was the second-warmest year on record for the United States and the warmest on record for the world. The graphs show precipitous rising just since I began the Daybook. I have seen some changes here: what have they been?

2017: Chronotope: January 21, Thaw (for the *Yellow Springs News*)

As I walked out the door at about 9:15 this morning, a cardinal sang and a robin whinnied. I drove to the Clifton Gorge, took the Rim Trail to John Bryan Park, came back on the Stagecoach Trail, maybe five miles, the air soft and still with a temperature in the high 50s.

Below me the river was fast, running up close to the top of the bank because of the recent rains, sun in and out through the trees, water cress bright in the strongest rivulets cascading down the slopes, a few hepatica plants showing, sweet rocket leaves, garlic mustard and waterleaf and leafcup leaves. Crows called and cardinals warbled. A buzzard drifted above me. As I returned toward my car, I heard a goose honking out its territory.

Today at a friend's house, an Asian ladybeetle was crawling on the inside glass of her back door. Two years ago, same day, flies emerging from the window woodwork and an Asian ladybeetle wandering the glass at the house of a different friend.

I saw no bluebirds, but eleven years ago today, Suzanne wrote me: "Between 3:00 and 4:00 p. m. I saw at least four Eastern Bluebirds in the South Glen close to the Butterfly Meadow area. Spectacular show."

In the yard this afternoon, I found a handful of pussy willows breaking out. Raking Osage leaves, I uncovered the fat sprouts of daffodils and the thin sprouts of hyacinths and precocious snowdrop sprouts, their tips already white. I found scilla seeds sprouting. Red peony stems lay at ground level waiting. Along the west edge of the property, the pachysandra was tall and green and fully budded. The lungwort had a few new leaves. By the last rose bush to survive the hard winter of 2014, chickweed was in bloom.

When I was about to go indoors, a storm came out of the warmth, three rolls of thunder, wind gusts and bursts of fat raindrops. A week ago, the koi in my pond lay still in the deepest water. Now in the storm, they rose hungry to meet me, ate for the first time since the middle of this past November (and for the first time this early since 2008).

2018: The thaw deepens, many of the sidewalks clearing, the stones of the garden appearing out of the snow. Woodpeckers steady, crows boisterous at 8:30 this morning.

2020: Hard wind and chilly on Big Pine Key in the Florida Keys. Melissa, the guest master, says it's just one of the fourteen winter days they get in a year. Much of the key was damaged by the Hurricane Irma, a Category 5, of fall, 2017, and only a relatively few houses survived or have been rebuilt in part of this area. We walked a mile or so around the neighborhood, vegetation taking over the places stripped by the storm.

2021: Clear sky, 33 degrees, light wind, the barometer having fallen sharply through the night (for the thaw), cardinals singing in the Phillips Street alley at exactly 7:28 this morning.

2022: Feeding birds this morning around sunup, I smelled a skunk, to the rattling of a woodpecker nearby.

Only when space and time are reconciled into a single, unified field of phenomena does the encompassing earth become evident, once again, in all its power and its depth, as the very ground and horizon of all our knowing.

David Abram, *The Spell of the Sensuous*

January 22nd
The 22nd Day of the Year

At times when our tether holds us on one small bit of the earth's surface, we tend to feel that in this little area we are seeing only fragments of life. In reality we are touching threads that run around the world. The smallest foothold on the surface of the globe places us in contact with the whole world's unending web of life. There are no isolated fragments. There are only threads and links and segments. Nothing is alone, nothing is unrelated, all are linked together.

Edwin Way Teale

Sunrise/set: 7:52/5:42
Day's Length: 9 hours 50 minutes
Average High/Low: 34/18
Average Temperature: 26
Record High: 67 – 1933
Record Low: - 15 – 1936

The Daily Weather

Between today and February 2nd, the average likelihood of below-zero temperatures falls from slightly more than ten percent down to less than five percent. And today is one of just five January days on which there is a better than 80 percent chance of afternoon highs above 30 degrees. A breakdown of the possibilities: 5 percent chance of 50s or 60s, 25 percent chance of 40s, fifty-five percent of 30s, fifteen percent of 20s and five percent of teens. Rain or snow is likely: 20 percent for the former, 45 percent for the latter.

The Weather in the Week Ahead

After the January thaw, the likelihood of cooler conditions increases briefly, making the 25th and 26th some of the crueler days of the month. And although the 31st can bring subfreezing temperatures 40 percent of the time, that day introduces a possibility for highs in the 60s for the first time since January 7th. Between the 26th and 28th, dry conditions prevail 75 percent of the years, and the 27th is the sunniest day in January, bringing an 80 percent chance of clear to partly cloudy skies. The 30th is the cloudiest day in the second half of January, with 70 percent chance of overcast conditions, and the wettest.

Natural Calendar

During the fourth week of January, the Season of Deep Winter comes to a close and the Season of Late Winter takes its place, often dominating the year until the third week of February. The Season of the Ten-Hour Days in Yellow Springs begins January 27 and continues through February 22, when the day's length reaches elven hours. The Season of Rising Temperatures starts on January 29 and warms North America until July 18, at which point summer averages reach their peak and then hold steady until July 29 when the Season of Falling Temperatures begins – and keeps cooling the land until the following January.

Daybook

1984: Deep Winter and record temperatures have frozen the ground for weeks. There's no green foliage at all left around the house.

1987: Cardinal sings at 7:39 a.m., r.

1989: Geese fly over honking at 8:30 a.m. Cardinals sing by 8:40 then get stronger in the afternoon. Doves heard at 1:10 p.m., the earliest day in the year that I've ever noticed them.

1992: Sweet gum seed balls half down, hawthorn berries half fallen.

1993: January thaw late and welcome. Rain yesterday and last night. This morning, low clouds, a light fog all through the countryside.

2006: Doves heard calling for the first time this year (like in 1989 on this date). Impatiens and coleus started in flats under lights this afternoon. Wren seen in the woodpile under the porch.

2008: The rose-breasted nuthatch came to the back bird feeder this morning. It must be staying through the winter here. One goldfinch seen at the sock feeder by the trellis. Only a few starlings are here today. Bittersweet berries, privet berries and coralberries hold on in the shrubs along High Street. No thaw in the offing.

2009: Crows flying over the house, robins chirping and even giving their singsong calls, cardinals calling, a nuthatch chirring, three starlings chirping in the white mulberry tree this morning between 8:00 and 8:30. Even with snow on the ground and temperatures below freezing for several weeks, it seems to me that spring is rushing into the village. Along the alley, winterberry hulls and leaves have been darkened by the deep cold of last week. Several Osage fruits have been eaten completely by the squirrels or raccoons. After we got home from Columbus (visiting the orchid show), I heard the bell call of a blue jay. On the way back we noticed a small skunk killed on the road near the dairy.

2012: Still no morning cardinal song despite the large number of males and females seen this week. Increased visits by the red-bellied woodpecker, the downy, and a small flock of starlings at the feeders.

2013: Four of the five daffodil stalks that were budded in the garden and that I put in water yesterday have opened all the way, are in full bloom on the kitchen shelf. Three fat robins seen near Fairborn this afternoon.

2014: John and Lisa reported half a dozen sandhill cranes flying over Dayton today, riding the hard, cold wind and snow.

2015: Crows at 8:00 this morning. At Ellis, no geese in the fields, but several large flocks passing through the area, appearing to look for the best sites to feed. Several geese across the pond honking and honking. At the arboretum oak grove: scarlet, sawtooth, swamp and shingle oaks have all kept their leaves, crisp and brown.

2016: Leah came by the shop today to report that when the weather had been mild during the first part of the month, hundreds of Asian lady beetles emerged from her walls inside the house, then died in a matter of days once the weather grew cold again.

2017: Crows at 7:38 this morning, temperature in the upper 40s, heading to 60 in the afternoon. Geese in the distance. A faint odor of skunk underneath my studio: spring. My koi seem to have accepted the thaw with gusto, came up to me and accepted food the first time since early December. (They were active and fed on January 8 of 2008, a record-breaking day of 64 degrees, but today and the 8th are the earliest I've recorded in the year.)

2018: The snow that lay six-inches deep when we arrived home from Florida on the 12th has almost all melted, and the high reaches toward 60 throughout southwestern Ohio. At 10:30, Michele Burns wrote from Flying Mouse Farms just outside of town: "I just wanted to let you know Flying Mouse Farms is tapping trees today. This is the earliest we have ever done it. Probably by about 8-9 days. John started working with a guy last year who sells maple supplies all over the region. He told John that most of the syrup makers are tapping in January now because of climate change. We have had 3 years in a row of bad weather so we figure it's worth taking the chance." Tonight, the first thunderstorm of the year, hard rain, wind, thunder, lightning.

2019: One starling seen at the feeder this afternoon, the first of the year in my yard. Dimi, though, had starlings at her feeders just a few blocks away last week.

2021: Doves heard at dawn. Wren "chrrrr" in the back yard in the middle of the morning, first noticed this winter. Michele from the Flying Mouse Farm tells me John is planning to tap trees on February 1, full moon time.

2023: About five to six inches of snow under the new moon and lunar perigee today, a few blackbirds joining the resident birds at the feeder.

For it is only at the scale of our direct, sensory interactions with the land around us that we can appropriately notice and respond to the immediate needs of the living world.

David Abram, *The Spell of the Sensuous*

January 23rd
The 23rd Day of the Year

Time only consists of the units of its measure. It can be defined by grasses instead of minutes, and with damselflies instead of hours, by flowers instead of days, with box turtles instead of years. Temporal value requires neither logic nor consistency nor numerical sequence nor social order. Our individual, arbitrary visions, deliberate or accidental, are the only true points of reference, and our private, scattered record of what we experience is the only history.

Alonso Byrd

Sunrise/set: 7:51/5:43
Day's Length: 9 hours 52 minutes
Average High/Low: 34/18
Average Temperature: 26
Record High: 69 – 1967
Record Low: - 18 – 1963

The Daily Weather
This is a pivotal time in the progress of the season: from now on, there is at least a ten percent chance every day of the high reaching 50. During the January thaw period (January 23rd - 26th), those chances rise to 20 percent. Other possibilities for today: 40s come 20 percent of the time, 30s occur 35 percent, 20s occur 15 percent, and temperatures in the teens or single digits five to ten percent. The chances of warmth are accompanied by clouds: 65 percent of all January 23rds are completely overcast. Rain or snow falls more than half the time. The temperature almost never goes below zero on this date.

Natural Calendar
The Season of Cardinal and Dove Mating Song coincides with the Season of Robin and Bluebird Migration toward the end of January, announcing at the same time the very first blossoms of aconites and snowdrops in the warmest microclimates of the Lower Midwest and the Middle Atlantic regions.

Daybook

1984: January thaw melts the snow.

1988: Large flock of starlings settles in the north lot.

1989: This mild January has already pushed spring as early as most people can remember. Cardinals began their mating songs today. Doves have been calling a week ahead of schedule. Janet Hackett telephoned to report that her yellow aconites are blooming. "And the maple tree is dripping, too," she said, "and you can see the white petals of the snowdrops. They're just beginning to open." Evadine told me her snowdrops were already open, aconites budding. Down along the Gulf coast, stimulated by a month of unseasonably warm winds, trees are flowering, says Jeni.

1993: A high-pressure system came through last night; clear this morning, one of two sunny mornings in 1993. As this high moves east, the wind will shift, come up from the south, guiding robins. A cardinal sang at 8:00 a.m., a long burst, maybe five minutes of song, then continued off and on throughout the day. This is the earliest I've heard that much cardinal singing. Worked outside until 6:00 this evening, still a little light when I went inside.

2002: Bob says he saw the first robin feeding outside his foundry window in Xenia today. A sluggish wasp walked across his kitchen floor as we talked.

2006: Cardinal singing hard at 9:00 a.m., doves calling. Starlings flocking north of Dayton Street, restless before the start of mating?

2008: Clear and single-digit cold under a full moon last night. Crows at 8:00 this morning, but no doves calling. Walking Bella, I came across a dead squirrel by the sidewalk – the same place that I found dead squirrels last year and the year before – although in March. I heard a cardinal quite a distance from the back yard in the middle of the morning. In the late morning, a tufted titmouse was singing, and one Asian lady beetle appeared on the south window. A large hawk waited for sparrows a while in the back white mulberry tree, then flew off.

2009: At the end of the two-day January thaw, I was working outside, was greeted by a robin at the woodpile. The hawk seen in the back lot this morning. Jeanie and Chris reported their predawn walk filled with constant birdsong. Rick called to say that he was at John Bryant State Park in the late afternoon, and he saw craneflies spinning in the sun and spiders weaving webs, with little hatches of bugs getting caught up in webs, and then a larger brown bug with wings landed on his boot, and he was amazed that "this close on the edge of this very cold weather these little things could be on the move so soon."

2010: Cardinals, red-bellied woodpeckers, crows, titmice calling this morning as the thaw deepens. I noticed that some of Don's daffodils were up an inch in places. One red peony stalk seen at ground level. Rick Donahoe called to report seeing one buzzard.

2011: Crows at 7:44 this morning, a cardinal singing when I went outside at 10:00. Starlings joined the crows feeding yesterday and today. Tat reports from Madison, Wisconsin that she heard a cardinal singing just after sunrise about 8:00 today.

2012: Warm south wind, 48 degrees this morning, hellebore buds straining, the south garden gradually filling with henbit (some with small buds), the circle garden with bittercress, the north garden with three-to-four-inch daffodil foliage, the porch bricks and the north garden with chickweed, the mild winter gradually allowing the ground covers to advance. Sparrows chattering, but no cardinals heard this morning. Ruby reports "snowdrops at white bud stage along Kyle Road," and "a big kettle of buzzards at South College and Herman Streets."

2013: Crows slept late this morning, 8:00 a.m. At the feeders, the birdseed is going down slowly, far fewer visitors, it seems, than in the fall. Now all five of the daffodils I brought in two days ago are blooming, apparently unfazed by having been frozen solid.

2016: Most bittersweet berries have fallen; a few hang on, like the crab apples beside them. Against the blue sky, the earliest pussy willow catkins show bright white in the sun. Starlings prominent at the feeders today. All across the East, heavy snow and wind, high tides at full of the moon.

2017: Most bittersweet berries, deep orange, remain on their vines. Ed Oxley reports fields of his snowdrops are in bloom. The mid-January thaw ended today with mist and chill.

2018: The euonymus berries have lost their red fruit. It lies scattered in the melting snow. The chickadees have been the steadiest feeders throughout the month.

2020: St. Mary's in southeastern Georgia: Maples are in red flower, small pink azaleas in bloom. The flowering maples became visible near Daytona Beach, then appeared and disappeared as we drove north. In Yellow Springs, Leslie reports a vast flock of maybe 2,000 starlings landed in her trees.

2021: Coldest morning of the winter so far, 13 degrees. Pure blue sky. Starlings at my window feeder this afternoon for the first time, but only crows calling, a few sparrows chirping near dawn.

2023: Melting snow. A half a dozen buzzards circle the north end of High Street. No robins heard since late autumn.

Journal

Camel crickets keep falling into my bathtub-shower in the coldest part of winter. Once there, they hop and hop, but they can't scale the steep, slippery walls that tower above them. Sometimes these creatures are small. Other times the trapped insect is mature and fat. According to my books, camel crickets can neither hear nor make sounds. They compensate for being both deaf and dumb by having unusually long and sensitive antennae. Young or old, their bodies are fragile but their reflexes sudden, allowing them to spring to the air at my slightest movement.

And they are obsessed with my smooth, white tub. They creep into the bathroom at night, mount the wooden tub-surround, and slip through the opening between the sliding shower doors. In the morning, I have to scoop them out, take them to the greenhouse, and set them free in the geraniums or begonias. Eventually, they find their way back into the bathroom.

What they are looking for who can tell? For the most part, camel crickets live in basements. They like the damp darkness of caves. The crickets I encounter probably breed in the crawl space under my house and find their way upstairs in the fall and winter seeking warmth.

But that is obviously not everything to know about them. Like the rest of us, they must have secret passions. They have evolved to succeed in a gloomy habitat, but one in which they are safe and nimble. What draws them to the sleek and fatal receptacle that will not allow their return? Why do they rashly throw their advantage away to explore the treacherous, shining bathtub in which they are helpless?

Are they are drawn to the whiteness of the porcelain like moths to the light? Does the bright chasm in the black night promise some forbidden pleasure? Is my tub the great and terrible temptation of camel crickets? Whatever their sin, I feel a certain comradeship with them. They should know better, but they can't help themselves. Their visitations confirm something I know about myself; I share some weakness with them, some deficiency of discretion, and neither they nor I know how to fix the flaw.

January 24th
The 24th Day of the Year

The good observer of nature exists in fragments, a trait here and a trait there. Each person sees what it concerns him to see.

John Burroughs

Sunrise/set: 7:50/5:45
Day's Length: 9 hours 55 minutes
Average High/Low: 34/18
Average Temperature: 26
Record High: 71 – 1943
Record Low: - 19 – 1963

The Daily Weather
The chances of 50-degree temperatures are 20 percent as the season of the January thaw continues. Forties come another 20 percent of the days. Expect 30s, however, 35 percent of the time, 20s or teens the remaining days. Odds for snow or sleet are 55 percent, making this one of the wetter days on Ohio's January palette. On the other hand, the sun breaks through the clouds at least one year out of two.

Natural Calendar
Late Winter typically occurs in early or middle January across the Deep South and in the Northwest. It comes during late January into February along the 40th Parallel, and in March east of the Rocky Mountains along the Canadian Border.

Daybook
1989: Cardinals singing by 8:00 this morning. Robin heard this afternoon.

1990: An hour walk at South Glen, quiet for miles up through the butterfly preserve, past the barn and up into Middle Prairie. March growth on the wildflowers, river high and strong. Coming back past Far Hole, I saw craneflies, then a small pale moth, then a flock of bluebirds and a flock of robins, the silence broken with their peeping. In the distance, blackbirds, then a chickadee up the hill, and a loud clear "tee-tee, tee-tee."

1993: Woke up this morning to a thunderstorm, hard rain, lightening. Another pivot to spring. Then the sky was getting lighter at 7:30, even with the thick rain clouds. To Springfield this afternoon: wind from the northwest and a long flock of crows along their migration corridor. Two flats of pansies started this evening.

2000: Crows come in at 7:34 a.m. Outside, there's a foot of snow on the ground, eight degrees above zero.

2002: A flock of crows, hundreds of birds, feeding in the fields near the freeway south of Springfield. They have not begun their spring movement.

2006: At 7:45 this morning, clear, 29 degrees, Venus low in the east at the start of her eastern residence, sparrows in full chorus, crows overhead, a small flock of starlings in the silver maple tree by the alley.

2008: An inch of snow over night. Crows at 7:45 this morning, a cardinal heard at 9:30.

2009: The robin is still peeping in the middle of the morning.

2010: Hard rain this morning about 5:00, an inch or so extra in the pond when I went outside, puddles in the alley. No pussy willows cracking, but the snowdrops continue to inch up through the mulch, and the deep red peony sprouts are becoming prominent. Cardinal heard at 9:30, but no birdsong except crows near daylight.

2011: Crows at 7:28 this morning.

2014: Deep cold below zero this morning, the crows staying away until after sunrise, no robins peeping, sparrows and cardinals subdued.

2015: Darkened leaves of euonymus vines fallen to the mulch below, berries gone several weeks ago.

2016: When I was walking Jill home this morning about 10:30, Cardinals sang out the whole way. Walking back, I heard a blue jay's bell call over and over along Limestone Street. Far away in New York City, a record snowfall of almost 27 inches overnight.

2017: In the middle of the afternoon, I drove under a kettle of buzzards roosting in a tree above Xenia Avenue (the main street in Yellow Springs), just a few blocks from downtown.

2018: Two crows were screaming and attacking a circling hawk this morning about 11:00. I stood and watched for a while; the conflict went on and on, and I finally went indoors.

2019: A news story from Bolinas in California reported that the monarch butterfly count this winter was just 1,156, compared to last years 12,360. In the 1980s, the number of West Coast monarchs was thought to be 4.5 million; that number was down to 28,500 at last count, possibly below the number needed to keep the population going.

2021: Cloudy, light wind, cardinals at 7:32 a.m. and then sporadic, doves two minutes later and continuing throughout my walk, crows at 7:41. With Ellis Pond frozen over, light snow and sleet falling, the geese are vocal, some flying back and forth, most hunkered down in the fields.

2023: Winter storm moving up from Louisiana. A murder of crows sighted after lunch. They were flying so high, almost, it seemed, the height of sandhill cranes.

Fer some queer folks
The robin is the surest sign of spring,
Fer some, it's pussy-willows,
Fer some, a bluebird's wing.
Er else it may be violets,

Er blossoms on the plum,
Er little frogs a-peepin'.
All these mean spring fer some.
But Winter's back is broken,
and Spring hez set her stamp
When we kin eat our supper
'Thout a-lighten' up the lamp.

Janet Stevens, "Fer Some"

January 25th
The 25th Day of the Year

My diary seems to be a journal of the wind, sunshine and sky.

Charles Burchfield

Sunrise/set: 7:50/5:46
Day's Length: 9 hours 56 minutes
Average High/Low: 34/18
Average Temperature: 26
Record High: 71 – 1950
Record Low: - 20 – 1884

The Daily Weather

The sixth cold front of the month arrives within a day or two of this date, and chances of a thunderstorm increase at the approach of that weather system. Today's high temperature distribution: there is a 20 percent chance of a high in the 50s, five to ten percent of 40s, thirty-five percent of 30s. Forty percent of the time, highs reach only to the 20s. Clouds cover the sky half the years. Rain falls 15 percent of the time, snow 25 percent.

Natural Calendar

Some almanacs say that the 25th of January is the traditional date for raccoons to mate. A different measure of the season: the Sun approaches a declination of 19 degrees today, putting it at its mid-November noontime height, and marking more than 20 percent of the way to spring equinox.

Daybook

1982: Pussy willows are opening up now in the thaw.

1986: Cardinal singing between 7:30 and 7:45 in this mild, rainy morning, the first time this year I have heard one before dawn.

1989: Cardinals and doves in full spring calling from at least 7:35 a.m. It's the end of Deep Winter.

1991: Cardinal sings at 7:30 a.m., then at 8:25.

1998: Cardinal singing at 8:30 this morning.

2000: A small flock of robins in the crab apple trees at the triangle park this afternoon. A few minutes later, a giant flock of geese, maybe a hundred in all, flew over the west end of town.

2001: Opossum killed overnight on Highway 68 south of the village. Late Winter movement.

2002: When I walked out the back door at 7:25 this morning, a cardinal was singing in the old apple tree. At Suzi's, the first dove of the year was calling at 8:30. At the front door, snowdrops were budding, and aconite foliage had emerged.

2006: Cardinal singing at 7:50 this morning.

2007: Casey called this afternoon to report he saw a huge flock of robins eating crab apples near the high school. At our bird feeder in the front yard, heavy feeding all day in the cold. A mocking bird came by but did not approach the hoards of sparrows. At the pond in the back yard, a flicker was drinking – the first time I've seen one this winter. Greg called at suppertime to say he'd seen a gull at the pond near the grocery store.

2008: Clear with deep cold near zero this morning. Crows at 8:00 a.m., titmouse calling at 9:30 when I walked Bella in the alley. Starlings are here to stay now, and goldfinches have begun to appear with more regularity at our feeders.

2009: Screech owl heard at 6:50 this morning. Cardinals and crows at 7:50, sunrise time. Full cardinal song at 9:55 when I walked Bella in the alley.

2010: Carolyn Treadway writes: "I saw a small flock of vultures, including both turkey and black, in the Northeast corner of the Morris Bean prairie, some in trees, some on the ground." Her note reaffirms the presence of both varieties of vultures overwintering in the area.

2012: First cardinal song of the year heard at 8:00 this morning.

2014: Hard south wind and snow this morning, sun this afternoon. I saw a fat robin drinking at the opening in the pond. Later, sparrows were bathing and drinking there. At Lawson Place, more sweet gum seed balls came down in the storm.

2015: First crows heard at 7:40 this morning, waves of the murder, groups up to a dozen each, crossing from northeast to southwest for several minutes. No cardinals heard. Heavy snow forecast for the East.

2017: Wild onion foliage four to six inches high in front of Jill's house and along the bike path.

2018: Sun and 22 degrees, cardinals (songs and chits), song sparrows, robins, crows calling and woodpeckers working at 8:30 this morning. At the feeder, the chickadees are common, back and forth, but the large sparrow flocks seem to have dissipated (for pairing up and mating?).

2019: After a thaw in the lower 50s, deep cold has returned. Casey called at about 3:15 this afternoon: "There's a couple hundred geese in the field east of Ellis Pond," he said. "They're hunkered down, soakin' up the sun."

2020: I just noticed that a branch on one of my jade trees had come into bloom.

2021: Cardinals, sporadic, by 7:28 a.m., crows at 7:32, no doves.

2023: The village is shut down from rain and ice, and snow covers Chicago and Madison, Wisconsin. But Jill just sent a photo of aconite buds, closed tightly, showing through a hole in the deep snow. This is the earliest I have seen them.

Spring is not yet at hand, but there is change, and there are subtle stirrings here and there, if we forget the calendar and listen.

Hal Borland

152

But now there are things to be heard if one is at all attentive. At noontime on a sunny day the dooryard sparrows begin to test a few phrases of remembered song....From the woodland the male cardinal whistles as though he really means it....True, these are slight matters, particularly on a day when the wind has a wire edge and the threat of more snow. But spring is the sum of many things, and weather is only one of them.

Hal Borland

Sunrise/set: 7:49/5:47
Day's Length: 9 hours 58 minutes
Average High/Low: 34/18
Average Temperature: 26
Record High: 67 – 1950
Record Low: - 11 – 1897

The Daily Weather

As the thaw season recedes, the chances of highs in the 40s or 50s also diminish to just ten percent each. Most 26ths are in the 30s (a forty percent chance of that) or in the 20s (a twenty-five percent chance), with a 15 percent chance of teens. After the passage of the next-to-last cold front of the month, skies often clear, and precipitation occurs only 25 percent of the years. The area's heaviest snowfall, however, occurred on this date in 1978. The 26th and 27th of that year brought the worst winter storm on record for the Lower Midwest.

Natural Calendar

On a chart of January weather, Yellow Springs lies along a line at which temperatures average 28 degrees Fahrenheit. That narrow belt of moderation reaches from Boston southwest across New York, New Jersey, Pennsylvania, Ohio, Indiana, Illinois, Missouri, Kansas and Colorado, snaking through the Rockies, ending up on the coast of Oregon and Washington.

To the north (except at higher elevations), average

temperatures drop approximately one degree every 30 or 40 miles until they reach the snowy zero of Lake of the Woods in Minnesota. South of Yellow Springs, averages rise at about the same rate, until they reach 60 near Tampa.

Once in a while, the Ohio Valley reaches the depths of Minnesota winters. Yellow Springs recorded 28 below zero on February 13, 1899, but that was the last year of such temperatures until 1984. Sometimes Florida highs in the 60s and 70s make their way into the region's January records. Most of the time, however, the Lower Midwest is at the midpoint from which the seasons advance or recede in relatively even segments.

Daybook

1982: Cardinal singing at 7:22 a.m.

1984: Walk in the thaw at Grinnell Swamp: Tiny leafcup leaves have survived the severe January temperatures, along with henbit, wild onion, sweet rocket, ragwort, periwinkle. Columbine is alive on the cliffs, moss bright green. Mint holds close to the ground. But the cress and a lot of garlic mustard have been hurt. A few berries of the climbing bittersweet have remained in their pods. Fragments of Osage fruits still clutter boulders and tree trunks.

1985: No thaw this year, four straight weeks without an afternoon above freezing.

1987: Cardinal sings at 7:22 a.m., a half an hour before sunrise. Heard cardinals at 8:30 and 9:30, too, a radical change from only a few days ago. Ellis Pond is still frozen over, children skating there this afternoon.

1989: Full song from cardinals, doves and even robins this morning. But no worms are up yet in the warm rains.

1991: The days are noticeably longer now, twilight lasting until well past 6:00 p.m.

1993: First tips of daffodils seen along the front sidewalk.

1994: Despite the cold, a cardinal sang at 7:35 a.m.

1998: Bell-like call of a blue jay in the back yard this morning. Then this afternoon in downtown Xenia, the first flock of robins I've seen so far this year was exploring the trees.

2002: Crows and cardinals at 7:25 a.m. Dove heard in the back yard at 8:35. Susi called to say her first aconite was blooming. A fat dandelion opened in the yard here this afternoon.

2006: Cardinal singing at 7:35 this morning. A small flock of crows came through as I walked the alley with Bella at 7:40. Sun and thaw continue – it's been a month now without serious winter.

2008: The first cardinals sang at 7:35 this morning, 20 degrees and overcast, a coating of new snow on the ground. A titmouse was chirping when I walked Bella at 9:30, and something like a flicker or pileated woodpecker was calling steadily as we went through the alley. This afternoon, I planted rainbow coleus in a flat, covered them and put them up on the attic landing.

2009: Only crows and squirrels at 7:30 this morning. Starlings were filling the North High Street trees when I walked Bella after 9:00. Today, Mary Donnellan wrote: "Cedar Bog had a huge number of robins last week. They are already in bright color. Cardinals are also in the bog and are gorgeously red. The tundra swans are back at Muzzie's Lake in Champaign County. Tufted titmice are relatively abundant."

2012: Coming back from the airport from picking up Neysa, we passed through the scent of skunk.

2013: News reports say that 2012 was the hottest year on record for the contiguous United States, a full degree above the previous record and more than three degrees above the average for the 20th Century.

2014: Mild today near 40 degrees, the snow soft and squishy. When I walked Bella in the middle of the morning, titmice and nuthatches heard along Stafford Street. A robin came to the hole in the pond ice again today.

2015: Three inches of snow overnight, major storm moving into the Northeast. Geese continuing to be restless, another flock seen around 9:00 this morning. John Blakelock called at 11:15 to tell me that about five minutes ago he had seen thirty of forty sandhill cranes circling above his house, and "then they took off to the southwest."

2018: Another giant, fat and beautiful raccoon caught in the attic last night, the second in the past couple of months. We let him go at Jacoby. He scampered away down to the river for a drink – having been caged up, full of a dozen marshmallows (as bait in the trap) for probably a dozen hours. A robin was rummaging around in the south yard this morning as I talked to Barbara in Idaho.

2019: Cold in the 20s and cloudy: I heard crows when I went out at 7:50 this morning, then cardinals started singing as I walked Ranger down Dayton Street. Then a blue jay sounded its bell call. Kat reported: "I saw four Eastern Bluebirds late afternoon today fly onto our clothesline today, sit for a moment, then move to a nearby tree and sit for a short bit then fly off. Beautiful! The blue and orange, not brilliant, but definitely noticeable."

2021: Freezing drizzle, barometer 29.65: The first cardinal in the Phillips Street alley sang at 7:29 this morning, and I heard the first chickadee "sweet-ee" song at 7:34. Now the daily entries accumulate through the years as a record of first birdsongs, as though little else was happening or mattered. The sounds of the cardinals, doves, crows, titmice, chickadees, blue jays sparrows become floating markers gathered together in the daily journal, connecting whatever particular day of the year, through the radii of memory and awareness, fusing all the minor events of days into one repeating mass of music, narrow, solid history of all the January 26ths or 27ths or 28ths or any day.

Journal

By this point in January, enough small changes have

accumulated, in spite of the severe weather, to mark the close of the second season of the natural year (Early Winter - the first, Deep Winter - the second). The third phase, Late Winter, is the anteroom to Early Spring, growing the birdsong that fills the mornings of March, rousing small mammals to courtship, closing out more of the old year's windfall seeding

Now comes the close of winter berryfall: the red honeysuckle berries have long ago fallen or been taken by birds. The orange fruit of the evergreen winterberry (euonymus) vines and the bittersweet vines has completed its planting. Hawthorn berries give way. Overwintering robins eat and scatter the crab apples.

Migrant crows join the resident crows. Juncos cluster, readying for migration north. Often riding the winds of thaw, flocks of starlings leave cutover fields to cluster in town, sometimes accompanied by robins and blackbirds. The tufted titmouse calls every morning, and the most precocious male cardinals cry out to set their territories before sunup. Owls lay eggs. Skunks and opossums look for mates.

In order to recognize the dramatic effects of these events, in order to turn the lean narrative of late January into spring, I look between the lines, drift off a little as I read.

In his book, *What We See When We Read*, Peter Mendelsund emphasizes the role of imagination in reading and writing, the transformation of the text into a new private entity through synthesis, reduction.

"This is how we apprehend our world," he says. "This is what humans do. Picturing stories is making reductions. Through reduction, we create meaning."

Having experienced spring before, reliving the rebirth through memory, I anticipate and fantasize. I tell a new story, stepping from one sign to another, making sense.

According to Mendelsund, the reader or writer is never completely tied to words. "Much of our reading imagination comprises visual free association, " he says. "Much of our reading imagination is untethered from the author's text. (We daydream while reading.)"

From a birdcall or fallen berry, the observer fashions the landscape according to the daydream. Then the seasons become imaginary constructs, personal projections, reconfigurations of past time into time to come.

January 27th
The 27th Day of the Year

How exactly good it is
to know myself
in the solitude of winter.

Wendell Berry

Sunrise/set: 7:48/5:48
Day's Length: 10 hours
Average High/Low: 34/18
Average Temperature: 26
Record High: 66 – 1916
Record Low: - 9 – 1936

The Daily Weather

The odds for sun today are the best of the month, the second-last cold wave of the month usually having come through. Eighty percent of the days are partly to mostly clear, and precipitation occurs just 25 percent of the years. The last time chances of blue sky were so good was November 13th. And the next time odds for sunny weather get so high is March 7th. Temperatures are in the 30s half the time today, with a ten percent chance of an afternoon in the 50s or in the teens. Forties or 20s each come 15 percent of the time.

Natural Calendar

Black walnut hulls are dark and collapsing at the touch of my heel. Only a few box elder seeds hang from their branches, thinning now like the honeysuckle berries. Tundra Swans sometimes reach Lake Erie this early on their migration north.

As January wanes, Orion moves more westerly in the mid evening, and to the upper left of that vast group of stars, past Castor and Pollux, the stars of Cancer follow. After Cancer, and shaped like a sickle, comes Leo, easily found since Regulus, now the strongest star in the eastern sky, is its leading edge. Early mornings in late January bring May's planting star, Arcturus, overhead. To the far east, the constellations of the Dog Days are rising: Lyra and Cygnus. Deep in the southeast, red Antares is glowing. Regulus leads Leo's Sickle into the west.

Daybook

1982: Pussy willow shrubs transplanted last spring were eaten off by rabbits this week.

1984: Flock of doves along Wilberforce-Clifton Road, flocking perhaps in anticipation of migration or mating.

1987: Cardinal singing by 7:24 a.m., steady, unbroken songs.

1988: No cardinals heard this morning in the yard, but Pat Dell reported flocks of them in the trees at their farm.

1989: Cardinal sings at 7:24 a.m. Robins all over the yard. Well, two robins. Moss is growing on logs lying against the fence in the back yard. Chickweed and dock are coming back at Jacoby. Buds on the multiflora roses have grown a fraction of an inch there. Daylily foliage is up three inches at the mill. Daffodils to four inches along the south wall, reports of eight-inch stalks in Dayton.

1990: Cardinal sings 7:55 a.m. Doves at 8:15. Purple deadnettle is budding in the warm winds. Possums are out: two killed along the highway south.

1991: Wilberforce: 3:25 this afternoon, as I was getting ready to leave the office, I saw a robin land in the ginkgo tree outside my window. A minute or so later, another robin. Then a third. When I pulled out of the parking lot, three more robins off to my right. After supper, Janet Hackett called: she had seen a whole flock of robins gorging themselves on the fruit still hanging to the crab apple trees in front of the library. It's spring!

1992: First robin seen in the ginkgo at Wilberforce at 3:27 this afternoon. Then a small flock there, then a large flock in front of the Yellow Springs library later this afternoon.

1994: Robin seen along Grinnell this afternoon, the first in a while.

Jeanie says she saw a bluebird near school today.

1998: Starlings cackling and singing at 8:00 a.m. John Zamonski says his tulips are up in Dayton. Here, the grape hyacinths are above ground by the water meter maybe half an inch.

2000: Small flock of juncos seen on the way to Springfield.

2002: Full moon, shrouded in wispy cirrus, setting this morning at 6:00. At 7:20, the yard was quiet, then cardinals and crows sang together at 7:22 a.m., the sky streaked with bright pink. A titmouse joined in a few minutes later, and then I heard doves in the distance barely audible: a full spring chorus.

2008: A cardinal was singing at 7:30 this morning.

2009: No bird calls this morning as a snowstorm bears down on Yellow Springs. Mary Donnellan replied to my question about the tundra swans: "They do not overwinter at the lake. They usually show up in January. They also show up at C. J. Brown (the reservoir about fifteen miles northeast of Yellow Springs), so I've been told. I haven't seen them anywhere except on Muzzie's Lake in Champaign County and a swale on Dolly Varden Road in Clark County."

2011: The first before-dawn cardinal song of the year today at 7:30 sharp. Crows came in at 7:40, titmice calling through the morning. I heard the first blue jay around 10:00. Starlings and sparrows dominating the feeders, and starlings seen in trees and fields on the way to and throughout Dayton. The northeast coast is being hit by yet another heavy snowfall.

2012: Only one cardinal call before sunrise so far this year, and this morning continued the silence. Although the sparrow flocks are loud through the day, no other birdcalls heard, in spite of the unseasonably mild winter. In the east garden, however, snowdrops were over two inches, white tips plainly showing, and many grape hyacinths and daffodils showing at least an inch. In front of Liz's house on Stafford Street, one snowdrop was fully budded and emerged from its foliage sheath (but still not open). A few gardens south of my yard, one aconite with its yellow bud ready to open. All around the village, great pools of water from recent hard rains.

2014: Spruce needles and redbud seedpods scattered on the snow by the hard storm winds over the past two days.

2015: Record Nor'easter batters Massachusetts as cold settles in over the Midwest. I saw the first starling at the bird feeder this morning. It apparently came alone, no flock nearby. A sign of the breakup of the fall and winter murmurations?

2018: Cardinal loud and steady at 10:45 this morning, light rain, cold front approaching. Walking downtown, I noticed a dead opossum by the side of the road, run over as he foraged in the night. I thought of the connection I imagined in 1993 between the first fly of the year and the first opossum roadkill.

2019: Twenty-five degrees and windy this morning, but a couple of geese screeched at 7:10. the crows were up at 7:20 and I heard the first cardinal at 7:29. Three large flocks of geese at Ellis Pond today; they are gathering for their Late Winter discussions and pairings. And at 11:40, Emily wrote: "I am at my outdoor sit spot as we speak, and I'm hearing from the hedge row by Vernet labs the 'cheer what what what what what what what cheat!' of the Cardinals spring song. Joy in my body, sun on my face."

2021: Walking home from Jill's at about 10:00 this morning, I heard the first blue jay of the year, along with the "chrrr" of a wren and the calls of crows and several cardinals.

2022: Mourning doves noticed at the bird feeder for the first time this year. Nor'easter threatens New England. At Ellis Pond, robin calls, and a huge flock of geese circled like sandhill cranes, then flew off.

Journal
On January 27, the day's length in Yellow Springs reached ten hours, which is 40 minutes more daylight than on

winter solstice. On the longest nights of the year, sunset occurred at 5:12 p.m. By February 7, sunset is 6:00 p.m., and the day's length is 10 hours and 22 minutes. At that point, the night is shrinking toward equinox at the rate of about three minutes every 24 hours, with longer afternoons creating most of the change. Last light in February's second week can last past 6:30.

Sometimes, it does not help to know the facts. When I am most eager for spring to arrive, the days are still too short. But when I have finally resigned myself to winter, the realization that the day is lengthening so quickly makes me pull back inside myself to hide from all the chores and responsibilities of the new season.

For all its limitations, winter hibernation gives me an excuse to be lazy and to procrastinate. This year, I have become a slug. I have started to love the dark night of the year. I have been tempted to go to bed after supper. I have even delayed looking at seed catalogs. The gray days and black nights have let me off the hook. They have encouraged my habit of denial. They have helped me to waste more time, and I have liked that. They have shredded my ambition, convinced me that my bucket list is just full of stress. Now I take naps, something I never used to do. I can sit much longer than I ever have watching birds at the feeder. I find existential meaning in the wood stove. I lose my way.

Then, sort of in the way sheep and goats know by the day's length when it is time to mate, I finally respond to the light. I know it is time, and I come out of my cave. I do pretty well for a while, order seeds, plant seeds, enjoy the daffodil blossoms, then the tulip blossoms.

Then, I get spring fever. I love the long day as well as the short night. So I just want to sit and watch birds. I want to sleep. I want to smell the freshly cut grass but I don't want to cut it. I want to put things off until tomorrow.

I lose my way again.

January 28th
The 28th Day of the Year

bf

Sunrise/set: 7:47/5:49
Day's Length: 10 hours 2 min
Average High/Low: 35/19
Average Temperature: 27
Record High: 66 – 1914
Record Low: - 13 – 1963

The Daily Weather

Today's high temperatures are in the 30s six years in a decade, and in the 40s or 50s twice in ten years, in the 60s once every two decades, leaving a little more than a 15 percent chance of highs in the 20s or teens. The likelihood of precipitation is low: just a 25 percent chance. Yesterday's 80 percent chance of sun, however, drops to just 55 percent. There is a ten percent chance of a below-zero low this morning, but this is the last morning of January in which below-zero temperatures are that frequent.

Natural Calendar

Two days from now, on the 31st of January, the sun passes a declination of 17 degrees 40 minutes, one fourth of its way to spring equinox.

Near this same day, a temperature pivot throws the entire northern and southern halves of the planet into reverse. And average temperatures start to rise throughout the country. Personal thermometers not only mark that process at home, but almost everywhere. And no matter where the starting point, the interval –

the rate of increase – is almost the same in every part of the United States:

During February, for example, the rise in averages at Columbus, Ohio is from 28 to 30 degrees. That interval is matched by Houston's rise from 54 to 56, Memphis' 42 to 45, Juneau's 25 to 27, Denver's 29 to 32, San Francisco's 49 to 51, St Louis' 32 to 35, Chicago's 26 to 28. In western states more subject to the vast thaws sweeping up from the gulf, the jump is four to five degrees: Minneapolis averages move from 12 to 16 degrees, International Falls' from 3 to 7.

These seemingly minor changes measure distance and time as well as temperature. If we actually can't see the days expanding by 90 seconds every 24 hours, even if we can't walk north now through green Louisiana, we still can know for certain that our Spring is underway everywhere north of the equator. It will reach us when it should, and we will pick our daffodils in the middle of an ordered sequence that begins this January week along the southern beaches.

Daybook

1988: Crows seem to be more common in the village now; at least they're louder around the house. Blue jays were calling at 8:00 a.m., joining the cardinals and doves. A sundog in the western sky this afternoon.

1989: Now the wild crocuses are up in the yard. Poppies are three to four inches and bushy. Robins have been loud all day. Blue jays at the bird feeder.

1990: Doves started singing at about 8:15 and continued strong through the morning. In the greenhouse, some mother-of-millions past their prime, some full bloom, some still budding.

1991: Cardinal at 7:50 and at 4:30, as I was going to work, then coming home. Two doves seen on Wilberforce-Clifton road, their activity picking up.

1993: Jeanie said dandelions were blooming on the golf course by the college today.

1994: Heavy rains have melted all the snow, the rivers are high and full of ice. The ground is still hard, the first time it's been frozen solid in what feels like years, probably since December 1989.

1998: Flock of juncos seen at Wilberforce. They are coming together to move north. This morning, starlings were whistling in the back trees by 8:00. The starlings are the first of the city spring birds, singing by the middle of January, the most optimistic of the birds. They begin the spring chorus.

2000: As I sit here working: a tapping on the cedar siding of the west wall. I get up and look out the back door. It's a red-bellied woodpecker with his red crown.

2001: When I walked around my yard, I found that some things were a little flatter than they had been in November. A few late Osage leaves, covered before I was able to rake them, were matted, sodden and dark. Celandine, lungwort, lamb's ear, parsley, and sweet rockets had all their leaves pushed akimbo. My neighbor's lily-of-the-valley foliage had been pressed to the ground by a storm, leaf tips forced to point east by the hard west wind. The snow had bent the New England asters and the white boneset, and now they were prostrate to seed the soil around them.

After just three mild days, including one sunny afternoon in the 60s, the land had reappeared as through winter had never come. The grass was still half green, just like it had been at Thanksgiving. The mint was standing tall and strong. The hellebores near our south property line had risen back to their autumn height.

Creeping Charlie was ruddy but creeping. Chickweed was bright between the bricks in the outdoor patio. Pachysandra was upright and budded. Garlic mustard had not been touched by all the weather. Blood-red peony buds still crouched in the peony garden. Waterleaf peered out from the mulch.

2002: At 7:17 this morning I went out side to wait for the birds to sing. At exactly 7:20, the first crow and the first cardinal called together. At Susi's, snowdrops were just about open, two yellow aconites with bright buds. Across the village, daffodils, snow crocus, and hyacinth foliage is pushing up. On the way downtown this afternoon, I saw two turkey vultures sailing over High Street, five to six weeks before their average sighting date. When I came back home, I went out to chop wood. As I walked to the woodpile, a ladybug flew by me, landing to sun itself on a honeysuckle branch.

2004: The deep cold of this January continues, but I noticed three flocks of starlings yesterday (after a week or so without one sighting), and a small flock of juncos when I was on the way to Washington Court House this morning.

2006: Another mild day, sunny, quiet, high almost to 60 at the back porch. Snowdrops budded, two inches high. Pileated woodpecker calling in the far back trees. A great blue heron flew over early in the afternoon. A titmouse was calling in the honeysuckles about the same time. Osage fruit now black and collapsing into the ground. Euonymus berries and honeysuckle berries almost gone. More daffodils coming up throughout the yard. New parsley foliage has appeared.

2008: Another morning with a cardinal singing at 7:30. A blue jay heard in the North Glen as I walked toward the Pine Forest with Jeff, a woodpecker in the distance. Two large flocks of geese flew over, one in the Glen, one in town. Casey said he's been seeing a Cooper's hawk in the neighborhood – that's probably our hawk, too – an immature one, according to the pictures I have.

2009: The cold January continues, this date much colder than most in my weather history. No cardinals at 9:00 this morning, but a flock of starlings close by. Casey called at 11:00 this morning in the middle of the heaviest snow of the season (ten inches on the ground already). He was watching four robins eating hackberry berries in the tree outside his window. He also mentioned that two red squirrels seemed to have taken up residence in his area, one more than I've been seeing here this winter. And a screech owl sits by its hole in a locust near the college science building when Casey goes by during the day.

In the middle of the afternoon, the snow stopped. A little sun. Total accumulation is a foot. Millions without power from Oklahoma through West Virginia. But I talked to Suzanne downtown, she'd been seeing "oodles of robins in the Glen."

And Janet Eubanks wrote: "It snowed, sleeted, and rained last night. And it was still snowing as I walked across the bridge to get the Springfield News this morning. It was early, but, light enough that I could see that there weren't any rabbit, raccoon or deer tracks today.

"Later, as I was watching the snow out my front window, my eyes caught a mink out for it's morning walk with its curved body and long tail lopping along the creek bank. Quite a contrast against the white snow.

"After it had stopped snowing and the drives were cleaned out, my friend called me to the back of the house where there were three pairs of cardinals enjoying an afternoon in the sun. And, as we were watching them, about 15 wild turkeys came down the lane looking for some lunch in the cornfield next door.

"Later, resting after a day shoveling, running the snow blower and with the help of a neighbor who came in to really finish the job, on the drive, there they were: three robins in my front yard. Then, my memory kicked in -

"I dug through the newspapers and told my friend, "I was right. The almanac said the robins would return on January 28.

"And, they did."

2010: Cold as the moon turns full. Birds quiet in the morning for the past few days, and no cardinals heard.

2011: No cardinals before sunrise, but the crows were up by 7:34, and the titmice were calling steadily. The blue jay was also loud after breakfast. Starlings visited the feeder. Snow cover continues – all of January with at least an inch or two on the ground.

2012: Crows at exactly 7:33 this morning, no cardinals or titmice or blue jays. Several chickadees and male and female cardinals feeding in the back yard through the morning, the Cooper's hawk stopping by to sit on the high feeder at 9:40. High 30s and hard wind through the day, sun coming out in the afternoon, so bright. In the greenhouse, the sun at 12:35 (the exact noon time for our longitude/latitude was 36 inches below the level I had marked on the wall on December 25, the day before the beginning of the second half of the year). In the north and south gardens, grape hyacinths are up at least two inches, and one daffodil is actually floppy it is so tall. This evening at 7:30, Venus was well up in the west, the first time the clouds have let me see it in its new evening star position in 2012.

2014: Deep freeze, just a small hole in the koi pond ice where the heater still wards off he cold, a robin drinking again today. Walking Bella in the Phillips Street alley, I saw that all of the bittersweet berries had disappeared, no sign of their hulls or fruit. Either the cold or the birds took them just in the past few days. At Nora's restaurant, Rosemary said her snowdrops were up three inches under the snow. Then she told how last week a great flock of starlings settled into her honeysuckle bushes and gobbled up all the remaining berries. "There was nothing left for the robins!" she said.

2015: Cold and clear, near zero. A murder of crows passed over the house starting at 7:35 this morning, continuing for about five minutes. No cardinals heard.

2016: Sunny and warm in the middle 40s. No cardinals heard before dawn (or after). Driving to Fairborn, I saw a small flock of black buzzards working on a carcass by the side of the road. Then I passed a sizeable flock of robins scavenging in a lawn, and then crows feeding in a soybean field. One raccoon run over on Dayton-Yellow Springs Road.

2017: John Blakelock called this afternoon, said he had seen a flock of about fifty bridled terns flying over Springfield. These terns have not been recorded in this area before, and John imagined they might have been blown off course or confused by mild spell of last week.

2018: Walk with Jill between around 8:00 and 10:00 this morning, 27 degrees, frost and fog to begin with, then the sun came through and thawed the sidewalks and roads. Cardinals were singing steadily throughout the village. Robins were common. We also heard song sparrows, house sparrows, starlings, crows, blue jays, doves and a red-bellied woodpecker. In the fields across from Ellis Pond (still frozen), hundreds of geese had gathered into three large flocks, were making a tremendous racket that we could hear from downtown, about a mile away. As we walked, small vee-formations of geese arrived and circled and landed to join the others, a congregation reminiscent of the great sandhill crane assembly I witnessed in March of 2013.

2019: Barometer dropping, storm and cold approaching: Walking down Dayton Street, I came upon a flock of about a dozen robins feeding on the fallen fruits of a decorative pear tree, the southeast wind scattering dry leaves around them. At Jill's, a skunk sprayed inside the garage.

2021: Twenty-three degrees this morning, cloudy, flurries: Cardinal at 7:24, Carolina wren at 7:25, mourning doves at 7:32, crows at 7:35.

2023: A short walk in the village: hellebores well budded, iris spears an inch or two, daffodil and hyacinth foliage two to three inches. This January has been mild, and the landscape is responding slowly, momentous changes quietly uncovered.

\

The well-being I feel, seated in front of my fire, while bad weather rages out-of-doors, is entirely animal.... Thus well-being takes us back to the primitiveness of the refuge. Physically, the creature endowed with a sense of refuge huddles up to itself, takes to cover, hides away, lies snug, concealed.

Maurice de Vlaminck

***January 29th**
The 29th Day of the Year*

*On my farm, drawn by the winter light
this gray afternoon of rain on the window,
I dream and meditate.*

Antonio Machado

Sunrise/set: 7:46/5:51
Day's Length: 10 hours 5 minutes
Average High/Low: 35/19
Average Temperature: 27
Record High: 66 – 1914
Record Low: - 10 – 1977

The Daily Weather

Today is often a windy day, usually much cloudier than the 28th, with chances against the sun rising to 60 percent. Rain or snow come one day in three. Temperatures are typically cool, with a ten percent chance of highs in the teens, 20 percent of 20s, fifty percent of 30s, ten percent of 40s and ten percent of 50s.

Natural Calendar

Cardinals, which sang only sporadically earlier in the month, have begun mating calls half an hour before dawn, doves, song sparrows and blue jays often joining their song. The first major waves of robins and bluebirds cross the Ohio River. On highways, roadkills attest to the increasing nighttime activities of skunks and opossums.

Daybook

1987: Cardinals and doves strong at 8:30 this morning. First thunderstorm of the year, hard rain later in the day.

1988: Sundogs in the afternoon (followed by temperatures near 60 the next two days).

1989: Temperatures near 60 followed yesterday's sundogs.

2001: Raccoon run over on Highway 72 near Springfield after two days in the 40s and a hard rain.

2002: Yellow snow crocus bud found against the south wall. Downtown: one purple crocus bud.

2004: A small flock of cardinals seen on the way home from school today. Jeanie reports that Don's mother (who is 92 years old) saw a whole flock of "red birds" around January 25th near Madison, Indiana.

2006: Chris reports several opossums run over this past week. Today is another day in the 50s with strong winds and passing rain showers. In the garden, I found the first tulip coming up and one wild mallow starting to grow tall – about three inches. Along high street, choral berries and the blue-black privet berries still hold. Redbud buds have started to appear along their branches. Cardinals now sing off and on through the early morning. The pileated woodpecker heard calling, too.

2008: Warm south winds and rain this morning. Crows, cardinals, titmice, and a flicker or pileated woodpecker calling after daylight.

2009: Silence and cold, a foot of snow on the ground, no thaw in sight. Then, as I walked Bella around 9:30, cardinal song followed me all through the alley. A robin was waiting for me in the honeysuckle bush by the front walk. And in the middle of the afternoon, a huge flock of starlings settled in the front yard eating crab apples and honeysuckle berries. This is the earliest in winter I've noticed starlings coming in to the village to feed.

2012: Titmouse calling at 7:40 this morning, clear and frosty, the first time we've heard it near sunrise this year. Crows well before 8:00. Strong odor of skunk at one point on the freeway as we drove south along the freeway about 8:30. My sister Tat and a friend of hers in Madison, Wisconsin have noticed flocks of cedar waxwings around their yards. The news reports snow owls in high numbers in Michigan, apparently expanding their range to the south. Hard wind all afternoon, sun and clouds, snow then clear. And in the middle of today's steady wind, John Blakelock sent a haiku: *Clipper zipping thru,/ blue interspersed with white squalls,/Lake Michigan's here!*

2013: Crows continue late: 7:55 this morning. In the alley, aconites are bright yellow, almost ready to open. In our east garden, two snowdrops have pushed up enough so that their buds, not quite spreading, are facing the ground. In the north garden, the first red knuckle of rhubarb is visible now. Near the pond, the red stems of the peonies have come up just a fraction of an inch, are starting their spring movement. All day, a strong southeast wind, warm in the 50s.

2016: John Blakelock reported seeing a bluebird today.

2018: Two very large flocks of geese flew over town at 8:45 this morning, honking and honking, heading north, perhaps to meet up with the geese that have already gathered in the fields across from the pond. Doves loud and clear on High Street.

2019: Deep freeze as a polar vortex drops into the Midwest, sending temperatures way below zero. Madison, Wisconsin at minus 30. At Ellis Pond, all the geese seem to have disappeared.

2020: Jill found Princess, the large silver koi that had been with me since 2012, floating dead in the pond this morning, the first fish I have lost in years. The pond is leaking somewhere, the water low; maybe a heron attacked him.

2022: From Madison, Wisconsin, Tat reports that her neighbor had a flock of robins in her yard! Along the East Coast, a Nor'easter is dumping feet of snow, snarling everything. High in my greenhouse, one stink bug is looking out the window.

All about me the snow thawed - the tracks of rabbits fell together and faded; the tunnels of mice were exposed; bird prints vanished. The air was sweet with the fragrance of thawing snow and rang

*with the songs and cries of chickadees, juncos, tree sparrows, blue
jays, the conversation of quail, the fresh vibrant cawing of crows
on wing.*

August Derleth

The first excitement of the daybook was a simple one. I saw a parallel to my own seeming lack of growth and change, I saw that nature was as deliberate as I was, that the movements I made in a day toward my purposes were as slow as the progress of a season; so, I thought, my seasons might, in time, take on the bright color, the clear direction, the sense, and the harmony of the year.

bf

Sunrise/set: 7:46/5:52
Day's Length: 10 hours 6 minutes
Average High/Low: 35/19
Average Temperature: 27
Record High: 63 – 1916
Record Low: - 10 – 1966, - 8 – 2019

The Daily Weather
Today's chances of totally overcast conditions are 65 percent. Snow falls 40 percent of the years, and rain comes 30 percent. Temperatures are typically cool, with a ten percent chance of highs in the teens, 20 percent of 20s, fifty percent of 30s, ten percent of 40s and ten percent of 50s.

Natural Calendar
I rejoice in the winter landscape, cut to the essentials. Earth and sky are more closely joined.

Harlan Hubbard

The first dandelions can be flowering, snow crocus and henbit budding. Sometimes moss is growing on logs. Sometimes tulip and grape hyacinth leaves are pushing out of the ground. Sometimes day lily foliage is up three inches, daffodil spears four to eight inches. When the sun is strong enough for all of that to happen, then flies hatch to warm themselves on the south side of your house, their soft presence almost tipping the delicate scale of time

Daybook

1986: After a mild few weeks, some new green leaves on the motherwort.

1991: An Asian lady beetle hatched in my office overnight. Outside, it's 30 degrees and cloudy.

1993: Starlings crowd to the new suet hung from the lilac. One gray nuthatch at the gazebo feeder, the first we've ever had. No early cardinal songs so far this year; they come for seed, but haven't started the territorial ritual yet. No robins seen or heard.

1998: Crows still flocking by the thousands near the Mad River west of Springfield. They've been here since late November, two full months at least.

2004: A sapsucker or downy woodpecker tapping on the siding this morning around 9:30. When I got home after a walk in the Glen, tired from working my way through the fresh snow, I heard a robin peeping in the front yard.

2008: Yesterday, the high was in the 50s, and the barometer dropped to 29.10. As I drove to Wilmington, the wind was hard from the southeast. In the night, it turned to the north, and the temperature was 12 this morning. Walking Bella, I heard titmice and cardinals.

2009: A cardinal sang again as I walked Bella about 9:30 this morning. At lunchtime, the back trees filled up with starlings. When I checked the front feeder, I saw a pair of cowbirds for the first time this year. The average arrival date for cowbirds in the Dayton area is March 1, but they have been known to overwinter here sometimes in the company of blackbirds.

2011: The first cardinal sang at 7:19 this morning, almost half an hour before sunrise, crows calling at 7:28, temperature mild in the 20s, sky hazy blue after a sleet-snow combination overnight. This period is part of the Groundhog Day Thaw, but it has been a cold thaw. More cardinals heard through the morning, starlings continuing to visit the feeders.

2012: Don Wallis, the mentor of all this daybook-almanac project, died today.

2014: I heard the first cardinal at 7:19 this morning, the Groundhog Day Thaw just beginning. Rebecca wrote this evening: "I went on a walk with Ruth in the Glen, and on the way back to the Antioch School, on the honeysuckle next to the driveway, we saw at least ten bluebirds! I've never seen that many bluebirds together. Beautiful."

2015: Very cold, wind, clear: Crows at 7:40, no cardinals heard (rarely call in the wind).

2016: Clear and in the 30s, light south wind, cardinals called on High Street at 7:19 this morning.

2019: Record-breaking cold throughout the eastern half of the continent. But a small flock of starlings appeared at my feeder for the first time this winter. Leslie reports a resident song sparrow and about two dozen cardinals in her yard.

2020: As I worked out in the studio this afternoon, I watched from my window as a robin rifled through the mulch for insects. Audrey reports aconites in bloom on the corner of Winter and Dayton streets today.

2022: Three large, noisy flocks of geese late morning, flying high as sandhill cranes, one going southeast, two going southwest. The Groundhog Day Thaw is beginning today, temperature finally rising above freezing. Robins peeping, woodpeckers tapping.

2023: I saw my first robin of the year in a yard on Elm Street. They have been so elusive since late fall. Geese have been loud and restless this afternoon.

The old year lost its power over me at some point in the middle of January. I felt rather than saw the change take place. Using inventories of what was happening in the landscape, I tried to define just what was involved in the disappearance of late autumn. I tried to understand just how something so obvious and powerful had eluded me. Where had it gone and how did it disappear?

After leaf drop, there was a lingering sense of the canopy, remnants reminding me of what had been there. Certain shrubs and trees kept their leaves longer than others. Their foliage trickled away during December, and then I became distracted by cold or snow. I experienced disbelief at the bare branches, and then a relief that the fall was over and that the crisis had passed. I felt a hardening of the heart, a hunkering down for the weather to come.

The number of honeysuckle berries dwindled after Christmas. Then, January stripped away so much time from December's nights, setting the birds singing and promising things they could not deliver soon enough. I instinctively looked for pieces of the new year, finally tiring of counting the old pieces. Pussy willows and the foliage of the earliest bulbs emerged ever so slightly. Little by little they all erased the loss of the previous spring, summer and fall.

Counting one thing is always about counting something else. The question of seasonal recollection asks me about something more, asks about passage and value and the shades of loss and reconciliation. In Deep Winter, I remember people separated from me like seasons (for whatever reason, because of transgression or death or distance), and I wonder about the perennial return of their images and the power of their continued presence.

Today is the gateway to February; almost everything lies below the surface, everything that has been and is still to come. My feelings slowly rise through the thaws and freezes and push me out into the sun of Early Spring.

January 31st
The 31st Day of the Year

In the woods we return to reason and faith. There I feel that nothing can befall me in life – no disgrace, no calamity which nature cannot repair.

Ralph Waldo Emerson

Sunrise/set: 7:45/5:53
Day's Length: 10 hours 8 minutes
Average High/Low: 35/19
Average Temperature: 27
Record High: 64 - 1917
Record Low: - 9 – 2004, 2019

The Daily Weather
Today's high temperature distribution: chances of highs in the 60s five percent, of 50s five percent, of 40s twenty-five percent, of 30s thirty percent, of 20s thirty percent, and of teens five percent. The sun shines on 70 percent of all the years on this date. Snow falls 30 percent of the time, rain 15 percent. This morning is the last of a series of four mornings on which a below-zero low is usually unlikely. Not so in '04 or '19, however.

Natural Calendar
The day's length is almost three-quarters of an hour longer than it was at the beginning of the month: sunrise just about a quarter of an hour earlier, sunset almost three-quarters of an hour later.

Daybook
1985: Snow fleas, the first time I've ever seen them, all over the snow at South Glen.

1986: Cardinals singing by 7:20 a.m. From my office window at Wilberforce, I watch two cardinals sitting in my ginkgo tree, fluffed against the wind. There are more, maybe half a dozen, out in the campus lawn

1989: A long thaw has held all the way through January. Robins, cardinals, doves are here and singing.

2001: Cardinal sang at 7:35 this morning. At Springfield, 10:00 a.m., I heard robins when I was walking across the field to go to class. I looked up: a small flock of robins in the maple branches.

2002: The first purple crocus opened in the east garden today. Daffodils are three or four inches tall, a few budded. When I took an arm full of firewood from the wood pile this evening, I was bitten by ants that had emerged in the mild day.

2006: Dianne Collinson may have seen the first wave of new robins; she called last week to say she had seen a whole flock in a tree near Tom's Market on the 23rd. Mike Miller found a clump of large, brown, unidentified mushrooms in his back yard last Saturday. Roger Lurie called on Sunday: "I was at Fort St. Claire in Eaton," he said, "and I saw a lone dandelion in full regalia. It was really surprising. It was the only one." Greg called on Monday to say that the pileated woodpecker had returned to his yard to nest and that the first purple primrose of the season had opened.

A Note for the *Yellow Springs News*: The average temperature for this month was 39.2 degrees, a full 13 degrees above normal. Although unusual for its even temper, this month was not the warmest ever. The January of 1890 reached 39.9 degrees. The January of 1932 set the record of 40.4 degrees. Other years that brought exceptionally mild conditions in January were 1933, with an average of 39.0; 1950, with an average of 38.4; 1989, with an average of 36.3; 1990, with an average of 37.1; 1998, with an average of 36.0. The January of 2002 had a relatively moderate 34.4 degree average, but, stimulated by several days in the 60s, aconites and snowdrops were ahead of this year's progress.

2009: The low close to zero this morning, wind chill almost 10 below. Robins twittering in the bushes before sunrise. Then the Groundhog Day Thaw began, highs to 30 for the first time since the 24th.

2010: A quiet Late Winter so far, a few cardinals and titmice singing after sunrise, once in a while a downy woodpecker and a red-bellied woodpecker will call, starlings whistling and clucking in the alley. Even though most of the snow is gone, the snowdrop progress has been stopped by nights in the single digits.

2011: Crows at 7:25, no cardinals heard early. An ice storm is moving in from the South, is expected to arrive tonight. This morning is cold in the teens and sunny, with high, thin cirrus across the sky and an east wind. The clouds thicken through the afternoon to altostratus, the sun so highly luminescent, and by 4:00, low and ragged stratus clouds darken the late afternoon. Light snow stings my face as I walk Bella about 8:00 this evening. Barometer falling very slowly.

2012: Sun and south wind this morning, 46 degrees. High of 61 this afternoon, just three degrees from the record of 1917. Along Stafford Street, many more of Liz's snowdrops have emerged from their foliage, hang down ready to bloom. A few houses south, the one budded aconite of a few days ago has become a mass of budded aconites. Jeff reports that a friend in Detroit has been seeing goldfinches in spring plumage for the first time this early.

Inventory at Jacoby this afternoon, the wind picking up, the sky clouding over. The river had flooded earlier in the month. Mounds and drifts of silt and sand followed the course of the high water along the paths, and the bottomland had a film of silt covering the foliage that has continued to grow: buttercup, chickweed, rocket, ragwort, wild onion. In the swamp, skunk cabbage was low but fat, many plants open and blooming. Gangly white stalks of last May's angelica crunched under my feet as I picked my way across the wetland.

The rivulets that passed through the cattail and grassy bogs were full and fast. I even saw small fingerlings swimming in one stream, far from any pool for safe haven, one water strider surprised in an eddy, watercress and duckweed there. Higher up on the hillsides, the ground was still muddy through the honeysuckle and box elder thickets. In a grove of black walnut trees, rotting fruits disintegrating if I touched them. Near the old springhouse, so many trees down, landscape of this year's storms.

At home in the yard, many of November's plants still holding their foliage: parsley, sage, rosemary, penstemon, lemon verbena, oregano, sweet William, yarrow, henbit, tall ragwort, garlic mustard, pachysandra, clematis, mint, primrose, coral bells. Bittercress is filling up the circle garden all around the new shoots of wood hyacinths an inch tall. The squirrels have shredded almost all the Osage fruits. Maybe a fourth of the oak leaf hydrangea leaves are still left, violet, twisted, one red peony sprout, a few budded chickweed.

2013: Goldfinches have returned to the feeders this past week (but still in winter plumage). Catherine says she has seen the same thing at her house. Today, the thaw ended abruptly with snow and the wind howling in the bamboo.

2015: Clear and still, ten degrees. First crows at 7:20 a.m. Cardinal in the honeysuckles giving the "chit" call. A wren and a nuthatch around 7:30. The main murder of crows came low over town at 7:40, and right after that I heard the first cardinal mating song, tentative, but clear, over toward High Street.

2018: Mild in the lower 40s, wind, sun and clouds: A goldfinch at the feeder, its upper body mostly gold. At the field across from Ellis Pond, the geese are so loud, maybe close to a thousand of them gathered, perhaps, for pairing and breeding.

2019: Faint odor of skunk in the house this morning, in spite of the temperature, nine below zero. Jill reports a large flock of robins, some in a tree, others on the ground in Delaware, Ohio, a little north of Columbus. And I came a cross a small flock of maybe a dozen in all at the Bill Duncan Park this morning. Starlings all over the north garden in the afternoon, and goldfinches more common.

2020: Crows active at 7:30, no cardinals heard. Michele Burns from Flying Mouse Farms writes: "I wanted you to know that we tapped on trees on Wednesday (the 29th) and the buckets are full to day. The maple sap is flowing! A good sign that spring is on its way." At breakfast, Jill mentioned that small ants have returned for spring on the bathroom sink. They have been appearing at the turn of the season as long as I can remember, but I've never noted them this early. Ed Oxley called to say he had been seeing "hundreds and hundreds" of crows gathered north and west of the village. He said he had also had a "poor male cardinal" attacking his image in Ed's window from morning to night, day after day.

'The month's average was 36.1 degrees, 8.6 degrees above normal, one of three Januarys above 36 since 1980. Precipitation was 3.83 inches, 1.12 inches above normal. In the circle garden, daffodils and some hyacinths have pushed up and inch or so.

2021: The month's average was 32.1 degrees, 4.6 degrees above normal. Precipitation: 2.82 inches, with about six inches in snow.

2022: Average temperature this month was 25.4, about two degrees below normal. Precipitation: 3.08 inches of water, about 8 inches of snow.

2023: Average temperature this month: 375 degrees, the warmest since 2006, and the second highest in the past 40 years, about 8 to 10 degrees above normal, three inches of precipitation, 8 inches of new snow. Michele from the Flying Mouse Farm said they had started tapping trees today.

Journal

Bluebird sightings complement other Late Winter events. At the end of January, John and Lisa (walking Clementine) saw a flock of bluebirds and patches of skunk cabbage pushing up.

The Eastern Bluebird is often a year-round residents in southwestern Ohio, but most of my sightings and those reported by villagers have occurred in January. The migration and breeding period for these birds occurs during this time, and collected January sightings create a seasonal mood.

From my notes:

January 1, 1988: South Glen, 25 degrees and sun: Three bluebirds seen up from bidge. Winter cress, thistle, mullein, and red clover are all bright green in the clipped field by the red barn..

January 1, 2012: Bluebirds reported in the Glen today, the same day I saw them in 1988: an overwintering flock or an early return?

January 14, 2014: In the afternoon, Liz wrote: "I have spotted bluebirds at Ellis this last week, several today and several at one of the boxes along the lane earlier this week.

January 14, 2022: Jack called to tell me that his wife, Jane, saw an Eastern bluebird in the Pine Forest yesterday.

January 16, 1988: The river is frozen all the way across beyond the covered bridge. But I saw a bluebird this afternoon.

January 17, 1994: Heavy snow and below-zero cold have shut Ohio airports, highways, schools. An eight-inch cover of snow throughout the back yard. But Marci reported seeing a small flock of bluebirds in the Glen.

January 19, 2019: Louise reports a small flock of bluebirds on Polecat Road near Ellis Pond.

January 26, 2019: Kat reported: "I saw four Eastern Bluebirds late afternoon today fly onto our clothesline today, sit for a moment, then move to a nearby tree and sit for a short bit then fly off. Beautiful!."

January 21, 2006: Suzanne wrote me: "Between 3:00 and 4:00 p. m. I saw at least four Eastern Bluebirds in the South Glen close to the Butterfly Meadow area. Spectacular show."

January 24, 1990: An hour walk at South Glen, quiet for miles up through the butterfly preserve, past the barn and up into Middle I saw craneflies, then a small pale moth, then a flock of bluebirds and a flock of robins, the silence broken with their peeping. In the distance, blackbirds, then a chickadee up the hill, and a loud clear "tee-tee, tee-tee" of a tufted titmouse.

January 27, 1994: Robin seen along Grinnell this afternoon, the first in a while. Jeanie says she saw a bluebird near school today.

January 29, 2016: John reported seeing a bluebird today.

January 30, 2014: Rebecca wrote this evening: "I went on a walk with Ruth in the Glen, and on the way back to the Antioch School, on the honeysuckle next to the driveway, we saw at least 10 bluebirds! I've never seen that many bluebirds together. Beautiful."

I have seen occasional bluebirds, and people have sent messages about them throughout the year, but January seems to either make them more visible or more desirable. Or maybe they actually are more abundant then.

Before you thought of spring,
Except as a surmise,
You see, God bless his suddenness,
A fellow in the skies
Of independent hues,
A little weather-worn,
Inspiriting habiliments
Of indigo and brown.

Emily Dickinson, "The Bluebird"

Bill Felker has been writing *Poor Will's Almanack* for newspapers and magazines since 1984, and he has published annual almanacs since 2003. His radio version of *Poor Will* is broadcast weekly on NPR station WYSO and is available on podcast at www.wyso.org. His three books of reflections, *Home is the Prime Meridian: Essays in Search of Time and Place, Deep Time Is in the Garden: New Essays in Search of Time and Place,* and *The Virgin Point: Meditations in Nature,,* along with the entire twelve volumes of *A Daybook for the Year in Yellow Springs,* are available from Bill Felker's website at **www.poorwillsalmanack.com**, as well as from Amazon.